On the Road to Tetlama

On the Road to Tetlama

MEXICAN ADVENTURES OF A WANDERING NATURALIST

JIM CONRAD

Illustrations by Kelli Glancey

Walker and Company
New York

With thanks to Alejandro and his family and friends; and in appreciation, to my parents.

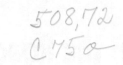

First published in the United States of America in 1991 by Walker Publishing Company, Inc.

Published simultaneously in Canada by Thomas Allen & Son Canada, Limited, Markham, Ontario

Library of Congress Cataloging-in-Publication Data

Conrad, Jim.
    On the road to Tetlama : Mexican adventures of a wandering naturalist / Jim Conrad.
        p.   cm.
    Includes index.
    ISBN 0-8027-1152-9
    1. Conrad, Jim—Journeys—Mexico.   2. Natural history—Mexico.
3. Naturalists—United States—Biography.   4. Mexico—Description and travel—1981–   I. Title.
QH31.C73A3   1991
508.72—dc20   90-21064
                                                                      CIP

Printed in the United States of America

10 9 8 7 6 5 4 3 2 1

Contents

PART TWO: WALKING INTO THE MOUNTAINS

PART THREE: TAMAZUNCHALE, AGAIN

■ CONTENTS

A Kentucky Preface

Gravel parking lot next to the Greyhound bus station in Madisonville, Kentucky: Somewhere north of here, the red-white-and-blue Greyhound bus is rumbling south on time toward me. Just four or five blocks from the hospital in which I was born, and twenty miles west of the little tobacco farm on which I spent my childhood, here I stand, a middle-aged American man, somehow needing to escape.

Though the plan is to go in a bus, right now I'm visualizing myself soon thrusting southward into the milky sky, soaring above hills and trees and the Mississippi River with its bridges. Flying out over Arkansas, from the sky I'll watch piny woods gradually give way to south Texas's mesquite plains and the Rio Grande; then, with northern Mexico's grayish brown desert spreading below, I'll break across the invisible but majestic Tropic of Cancer. Finally, feeling within myself a singing and dancing, I'll descend and simply immerse myself inside that shimmering, oversimmered, too-spicy, and maybe—yes, I *hope*—slightly disreputable stew of central Mexico.

A side-glance at my dark, almost transparent reflection in the Greyhound building's picture window shows me standing alone, tall, slender, stiff, wearing sunglasses, and with an expressionless, bearded face. My own dry image projected amid Mexican fantasies shocks me; indecisively I shuffle my feet and the three surrounding tall concrete-and-glass walls amplify atonal, crunched-gravel sounds.

Am I really the man to go to Mexico on behalf of such a half-baked deception?

For the plan is to arrive there—there in Tamazunchale in the central Mexican state of San Luis Potosí where my friend Alejandro lives—announcing the lie that I wish to write a book about the area's natural history.

But, the fact is, mostly I'll just be be a meddler, indulging in what I suppose to be the spirit of Goya exiled at Bordeaux, Gauguin escaped to Tahiti, and John Coltrane being himself . . . me, there in Tamazunchale, somehow connected to this Prufrockian reflection now beside me.

At age forty-two, you see, identifying and categorizing plants and animals no longer is enough for this college-educated professional naturalist. Beholding things natural does still fascinate and inspirit me, you understand; it's just that somehow now I must have a summer of anarchy and sensuality to fill up this calm interior that for a long time has grown within me empty, eggshell-like.

The bus comes. Here are the first lines I write in my notebook:

July 20

1:20 P.M.	Leave Madisonville, Kentucky, on Bus #6591
4:50 P.M.	Leave Nashville, Tennessee, on Bus #4778
10:00 P.M.	Leave Memphis, Tennessee, on Bus #1351

July 21

9:50 A.M.	Leave Dallas, Texas, on Bus #KG 231
6:30 P.M.	Arrive Laredo, Texas
7:05 P.M.	Walk across bridge into Nuevo Laredo, the state of Tamaulipas, Mexico

8:30 P.M. Leave Nuevo Laredo on Estrella Blanca bus
line

July 22

12:45 A.M. Leave Monterrey, the state of Nuevo León, on
Transportes del Norte bus line

6:30 A.M. Leave Ciudad Victoria, the state of Tamaulipas,
on Oriente bus line

9:00 A.M. Leave Ciudad Valles, the state of San Luis Potosí, on Sistema Vencedor Golfo bus line

11:45 A.M. Arrive Tamazunchale, San Luis Potosí
(N 21°17'50", W 98°47'18")

Part One

Beneath the Cocuite Tree

Música Tropical

Up slope, that rooster—just from its voice I know it's a fat, red-feathered cock, with eyes all lazy and arrogant. Down slope, *that* rooster's crowing is sharp and tightly packaged and I'll bet he's a glossy black bantam. So, cock-a-doodle-doos from everywhere, one after another and rolling together, almost harmonizing, hundreds of them, and me here with my eyes closed, laughing, laughing . . .

I'm lying on Alejandro's broken cement porch floor, and this moment at dawn is the most exquisitely stereophonic moment of my life!

With the sky above the valley lighting up, the ongoing, superimposed cock crowings calm down a little. Then, on cue, like cymbal crashes among flurries of violin staccato notes, random turkey gobbles begin. Each gobble—they erupt about every ten seconds—is both powerful and funny sounding; outrageous, but also somehow perfect for this precise moment and place.

Minutes pass and now somewhere down slope a goat starts bleating, begging piteously; the mammalian sincerity in its voice makes those earlier calls of roosters and turkeys sound mechanical and one-dimensional. Inside Alejandro's house a little girl starts coughing, for the morning is cool and the air is heavy with wetness. The child's homey-sounding croupings bring on a whole new panoply of feelings, so that now even the goat's cry seems impersonal and irrelevant and the cacophony of rooster and turkey calls becomes mere background noise.

Three or four lots down slope somebody turns on a radio. It's *música tropical* with the volume turned so high that the sound comes out distorted. The lyrics are mostly unintelligible; the words are repetitive, with the phrase *la bamba* being repeated at least fifty times.

Just beyond the porch's tin roof above me, tonguelike banana leaves, ten feet long and two feet wide, arch glowingly warm green beneath the milky sky; a large stalk of green bananas on a crooked stem emerges from where the big leaves' petioles unite. Nearby stands a twenty-foot guava tree loaded with spherical, green, pecan-size fruits. Near the top of a ten-foot papaya, two-foot-long, yellow-orange fruits cluster together; a nonflowering royal poinciana fills up the rest of the sky with broad, feathery, twice-pinnate leaves; on the plot below, six thirty-foot mango trees rise with dignity, abundantly adorned with baby-head-sized fruits silvery green below and burgundy red above, dangling heavily on fifteen-inch, cordlike, leafless stems.

All these trees and bushes are glossy wet with the night's rains, and this is what I see as I sit leaning cross-legged against the gray cinder-block wall of Alejandro's house, gazing across the densely populated valley below—that part of Tamazunchale called Colonia el Sacrificio.

Now more radios open up and two or three species of tropical birds begin calling. Someone methodically pounds on

4

something sounding like a metal barrel; this noise goes on and on and who knows what that person is doing? A dog starts barking, diesel trucks begin passing through town below, and the cool, wet air becomes suffused with odors of refried black beans, hot tortillas, and green chili peppers being ground for hot sauce. Alejandro walks stiff-legged onto the porch.

"*Buenos días*," he says, smiling sheepishly and bending down to shake my hand.

Nest of Leaves

On the slope next to Alejandro's, years ago Epifaño Castañeda excavated a twenty-by-thirty-foot plot of level ground. Using a pick and shovel he dug down through shaley sandstone; today he shakes his head telling how hard the work was. For some reason Epifaño never built a house there, so now I pay him a month's rent for the plot.

He asks a price that in the United States would pay for a single movie and one hamburger. Later Alejandro grimaces and says that I've paid too much. However, I'm content, for Epifaño is a hard-working man barely getting along. He operates a small garage (tin roof, dirt floor, and two walls of white-painted bamboo stems) beside the Pan American Highway, which runs right through Tamazunchale.

Beneath a black-locustlike tree that Alejandro calls *cocuite* (it's *Gliricidia sepium* of the bean family), on Epifaño's plot, I erect my two-man, green-and-white backpacker's tent, then dig a trench around it for catching rainwater. Here I'm far enough from Alejandro's house for privacy but close enough for us to talk through the twenty-foot-high, diffuse wall of shrubs and weeds rising between us.

Already I see that for Colonia el Sacrificio's kids I'll become this slope's main oddity, the very place to go when things get dull. This afternoon I'm visited by Martha (pronounced *Marta*), Nanaya, Janet (ya-*net*), and Conchita. They're between three and eight years of age.

Three-year-old Conchita tears leaves from low-hanging cocuite branches and methodically drops them into a nestlike basin formed by four cantaloupe-size rocks at the base of one of Epifaño's rock walls. The mangled cocuite branches emit a powerful, wet green odor that fills the hot air pooled in the tree's shadows. The children's voices are soft and musical, and their manner of laughing and moving among the shadows is magical.

Sitting on a rock just beyond the children's circle, I realize that I've been feeling like dry and wadded-up scrap paper;

now I'm soaking up a hundred kinds of moistness. Somehow I have needed this.

Janet says that Conchita is ill. In describing the disease she uses a word I've never heard and that doesn't occur in my Spanish dictionary. When I ask her what it means, she says, "Oh, it means that she's going to die pretty soon. She falls down and can't breathe, and her lips turn purple." Conchita hears this, purses her lips, and looks at us with the indomitable look of a three-year-old. Then she lays another handful of green cocuite leaves into her pungent nest among the jagged rocks.

The Spring

Eight-year-old Martha and I head for the spring to wash my clothes and fetch a bucket of water. Martha is Alejandro's granddaughter and the daughter of Paulina. The spring lies about ten minutes away, just across Tepetlayo Ridge. The dirt path leading there is fine when dry but very slippery when wet. This morning a drizzle is falling.

The trail is so narrow that as we walk my shoulders brush both of the five- to ten-foot-high vertical walls of weeds and shrubs alongside us. The vegetation is warm green and shining with wetness; above us hang a dark gray sky and blue-green mountains.

At the spring three women wash clothes while their naked children bathe. When I arrive everyone stands and stares at me with faces showing curiosity, a little wariness, and not the least embarrassment that I see them staring. I ask Martha to choose for us a good clothes-washing place. She leads me to the stream's edge where there's a large flat rock worn smooth on top by generations of clothes washers.

Standing in the stream's water she demonstrates how to

wet the clothes, sprinkle them with dry soap powder, and then, while anchoring the bottom of the garment in the left hand, with the right hand move the top part up and down across the stone, working up a good suds. After some practice I assume that I'm doing as well as anyone, but then I hear the women and children laughing, and Martha says that maybe I'd better let her take over. She and I finish together.

After rinsing the clothes, the drizzle becomes a general rain and the darkest cloud heaped against the highest southern peak begins rumbling. Martha wants to go home, but I feel like wandering around.

Except for the few huge trees right around the spring, all big trees on this side of Tepetlayo Ridge have been felled and replaced by weeds and bushes. These giants around the spring cause the washing place to be a cool, moist, deeply shaded park. One of the largest trees is a ceiba, with a buttressed trunk about five feet in diameter, growing straight up and slightly bulging at about the ten-foot level. Another is a strangler fig. Beneath its branches the ground lies thickly strewn with spherical, red-skinned figs not quite half an inch in diameter. These trees' larger, lower branches are festooned with gardens of bromeliads, mosses, and ferns; thick, leafy stems of climbing members of the arum family shroud much of the big trees' trunks.

Here and there white limestone emerges from the ground; rocks next to the stream are covered with a wet, green carpet of selaginella, moss, and liverwort. Along the stream grow several species of fern, some with frilly, lacy fronds and others with broad leaves looking as if they've been cut out by a child with round-pointed scissors. Several arums of the kind used in potted plant arrangements in the United States grow here abundantly, especially a species with deep green, glossy, arrowhead-shaped blades.

Lifting my face toward the big ceiba's canopy I see large raindrops full of bright silverness falling as if in slow motion. While I stand here enchanted, again the women and children start laughing; Martha, a little embarrassed, suggests that the storm is too close and we should go home.

From a special pool kept free of the main stream's soap-suds, we dip sparkling water into our plastic bucket, observing the rule that the bucket itself shall not be dipped into the spring; a plastic bowl must be used for ladling. A young woman with a Virgin Mary look on her face and lugging her own large bucket of water approaches me:

"Señor, will you please place this bucket atop my head?" I do, and she walks away smiling demurely.

Martha and I follow her, I clumsily shifting my own bucket from hand to hand and Martha giggling.

11

Friendliness of Trees

Standing on Alejandro's porch overlooking the valley of Colonia el Sacrificio, here and there tin roofs appear, but, more than anything, I see trees. It seems impossible that beneath this slope's trees such a high population density maintains itself. Most family plots, which occupy every inch of this slope, are reached by muddy footpaths; the plots themselves average about fifty by seventy-five feet; nine people live in the two-room shack on Alejandro's plot, and that's about average.

Besides abundant cocuite trees (the species sheltering my tent), several other fast-growing, rather brittle, pithy trees are common here. The most common are a species apparently in the elm family and "naked Indian trees" (*Bursera simaruba*, also called gumbo-limbo), with smooth, reddish bark. Somehow these weed-trees survive and thrive, despite never-ending onslaughts by kids who rip off branches for building play huts and swatting butterflies, of young men with machetes who hack tree trunks randomly just to have something to do, and of landowners who during occasional spurts of energy "just cut everything down."

Maybe a third of the valley's tree cover comprises fruit trees, especially those bearing oranges, lemons, mangoes, guavas, papayas, and bananas. Coffee shrubs often are planted in the shade of taller trees. Seldom do this slope's fruit trees grow in regular straight-rowed orchards; mostly they seem to have been planted randomly and without much forethought about how the mature trees would affect their immediate surroundings or how the trees' fruits would be harvested.

This haphazardness and richness of fruit trees stands in harmony with the slope's randomness of wandering pigs, turkeys, and chickens; its randomness of types of people brought together only by their inability to afford living elsewhere; its randomness of bird calls and radio music and children laughing and of sounds of diesel trucks and buses on the highway below; its randomness of crooked, unplanned

13

trails that in one place may be nothing but a slick outcrop-
ping of well-worn limestone or a trench cut through mud,
but in another a ten-foot-wide, politician's delight, concrete
sidewalk sloping upward at twenty-five degrees. Somehow
these trees help me feel at home. Something about this
unique kind of forest strikes me as being exceedingly . . .
friendly.

However, this slope with its friendly trees doesn't extend
far beyond this valley. Below, exit the valley of Colonia el
Sacrificio through the one-laned street called Callejón del
Aguacate (Avocado Alley) and the world instantly changes to
little grocery stores, hardware stores, funeral parlors, government buildings, restaurants, street vendors with kiosks and
pushcarts, banks, the church . . . and a few street trees and
weeds along the sidewalks.

In contrast, on top of Tepetlayo Ridge above us runs a footpath that quickly passes beyond Colonia el Sacrificio's special
forest into a landscape dominated by hillside pastures rank
with weeds, a few fields of corn and nopal (an edible cactus),
and former fields and pastures reverting to secondary forests.
In a few places where the slope is extremely steep, semima-
ture forests rise filled with viney members of the arum family, bromeliads, orchids, peperomias, and birds that aren't
found in weedy places.

This footpath intrigues me. Mostly it's used by country
people — Nahuatl-speaking Indians — living in the mountains
off the main road. A never-ending parade of Nahuatl speakers
carry on their backs and heads things they want to sell in
Tamazunchale's markets. Usually the men speak enough
Spanish for us to converse, but most of the women know
only Spanish numbers and a few market words.

This morning as I went birdwatching along the footpath,
a man dark with sweat and mud, smelling mightily of wood-

14

smoke and carrying over a hundred pounds of firewood on his back, stopped, smiled at me, and said, "Señor, would you care to buy a chicken?" He saw that I was caught off guard, so quickly he added, "I have a hen here in the bag under my arm. . . ." Farther on another man invited me to buy roasted coffee beans.

Thus now I have identified at least three very distinct zones of vegetation. And something tells me that later I shall explore much more of this path on top of Tepetlayo Ridge—this trail that leads into the mountains, where the Nahuatl speakers live.

Nose Walking

■ Awaken. Odors of the night's rains pooling in the co-cuite's shadows, of mud and of my wet, water-repellent nylon tent.

■ Climbing to Alejandro's porch I pass the outside toilet with its ripe bouquet of robustly earthy, almost breathtaking exhalations. This odor reminds me of the outdoor toilet I used as a child on the Kentucky farm . . . my mother's purple-blossomed clematis abundantly overgrowing the white-washed trellis, the toilet itself constructed of heavy bald cypress boards, whitewashed and smelling of lime. . . . How strange to be visited by these homey recollections now, in this exotic landscape.

■ Sipping coffee with Alejandro I tell him that in the States I don't drink coffee because of the caffeine, so before I develop the habit here I'd better stop drinking it; from now on, each morning I'll be happy with nothing but a cup of hot water. Alejandro slips from the porch and climbs down the weedy embankment below us. From a dense, yard-high clump of grass looking like robust fescue he tears a foot-long section of leafblade and caries it back, crushing it in his hand.

I smell it. Ah, it's lemongrass, *Cymbopogon citratus.* He calls it *zacate limón* and says that from now on during my morning visits I can drink zacate limón tea.

■ At 9:00 A.M. it's warming up fast and onto the porch the day's first breezes bring married odors of hot tortillas, refried black beans, and wet chicken manure.

■ As Alejandro, Martha, and I descend the slope we pass dozens of Colonia el Sacrificio's plots, each different from all the others and each engaged in its own rituals. Around one, the odor of woodsmoke is strong; from the next comes the sweet smell of a blossom we can't find; from another issues the greasy odor of frying pig flesh; at the next there's a strong odor like that of cucumbers, but Alejandro says that nobody here would have cucumbers.

■ Leaving Avocado Alley and walking onto the street, we're flooded with fumes of diesel engines and the odors of mud, a passing woman's perfumed talc, rotting fruit, and dog shit.

■ Even before hearing the sharp squeaks of the ten-foot-long, dark, almost worn-out, greasy machine used to crank out hot tortillas every morning, we smell the hot, heavy, doughy tortilla odor twenty yards down the street from the Super Tortilladora.

■ At the municipal market's entrance, women with long black braids wearing single-piece dresses of the brightest colors sell orange mushrooms and live freshwater shrimp, both with their own odors. Inside the market we find too many fruits, vegetables, spices, herbs, leather goods, and freshly constructed wooden articles to describe, and each thing has its own odor, which mixes with all other smells to form a single pungent, pooling-on-the-concrete-floor presence. Approaching the back stairs leading to the market's second level

we skirt the meat stalls, passing through the unctuous odor of warm, naked, dismembered, raw flesh.

Stepping onto the second level, we pass a great wooden tray of dried, black sweet peppers that smell like cumin. Now before us rises an eight-foot-high altar to the Virgin of Guadalupe. A two-foot-high statue of the Virgin is surrounded by flickering candles and bouquets of several kinds of flowers. Behind the altar we stand looking over the building's low cinder-block wall onto the Rio Moctezuma below; swollen by recent rains, its waters are brown and fast-moving and tug at the green wall of weeds and small trees along its banks. Yellow butterflies flit all along those green walls. Standing here I smell mud, raw flesh, pig manure, and burned candle wax.

The View from Tepetlayo Ridge

From Tepetlayo Ridge atop Colonia el Sacrificio's southeastern slope, the hills toward the east are unimpressive; however, one senses beyond them the presence of broad, flat lowlands. In contrast, toward the northwest, the view is soon blocked by high, blue-green ridges and peaks. Each morning these peaks are cloaked with low clouds; along certain ridges and passes, great sheets and blocks of cloud build up, held there by invisible temperature and humidity gradients.

Far beyond my line of vision toward the east lies the Gulf of Mexico. At this latitude, prevailing winds come from the east, from off the Gulf, so the winds I'm feeling right now made their landfall just south of the port city of Tampico. Then they coursed across low, flat land where tropical forests have been replaced by vast fields of sugarcane, immense and weedy pastures on which graze white, humpbacked cattle called zebu, and little towns of a flavor not unlike Tamazunchale's.

When the winds arrive here, they hit the green-sloped peaks behind me—those peaks with names like Soyotla, Tlazuapa, San Miguel, San José, Mixquetla, and Acontla. But these peaks really are just foothills.

If right now we should get into a car in Tamazunchale and on the two-lane Pan American Highway drive south for about ten minutes, we'd come to a spot where the road starts climbing as if it were embarking up a gigantic wall; before long the air rushing through our car's windows would feel much cooler, drier, and thinner than what we feel here. When the road reaches the wall's top, instead of beginning a long descent back into lowlands, it would level out; for the rest of our trip to Mexico City we'd run across that jacked-up region between the eastern and western Sierra Madre Mountains called the *altiplano.*

When the Gulf's hot, moisture-laden, westward-flowing air reaches Tamazunchale, it begins rising in order to flow onto the altiplano. As the air rises it cools, and since cool air can't hold as much moisture as hot air does, rain falls. . . .

In fact, each afternoon since my arrival, impressive thunderstorms have formed above Tamazunchale, dumping very much rain and setting off spectacular displays of lightning and thunder. These storms cool things off; they also cause this slope's trails to be treacherous. The mud that forms on top of this region's limestone is puttylike and slick.

The barefoot Nahuatl-speaking men and women on the footpath on top of Tepetlayo Ridge . . . I wonder whether they can think of these storms in the expansive, geographical manner I've just described or whether to them storms are just storms . . . or maybe something else that I can't even imagine? I wonder which of us regards the storms with the greater awe?

Alejandro's Nahuatl

During the first years of our friendship, Alejandro always told me that he could understand only a little of the Nahuatl language — a language belonging to the Uto-Aztecan linguistic stock, which includes Comanche, Kiowa, Pima, Papago, and Hopi. When years ago I first met Alejandro, he told me that as a child he had spoken Nahuatl, but when he moved into the lowlands and began speaking Spanish he simply forgot his native language. During recent years, however, he's proved that he remembers a lot. During my last two visits, he's taught me many Nahuatl names for plants and animals.

Yesterday as we were walking through the market, we found a stall selling cheap comics, school supplies, and Bibles. One set of bilingual Bibles was organized with parallel texts, with each page bearing Scripture written in Nahuatl above and Spanish below. These Bibles were very inexpensive so I bought one for Alejandro, suggesting that he might brush up on his Nahuatl.

In the afternoon, back on the porch, he began reading in his put-the-finger-on-one-word-at-a-time manner. Immediately he realized that the Nahuatl he speaks is of a dialect different from the one used in the Bible; for over an hour he never stopped laughing at the Bible translator's Nahuatl.

This afternoon as I sit typing on a rock beside my tent, Alejandro comes for a visit. He kneels beside me and from a paper bag presents me with some saltines and a seventy-three-page pamphlet with the title (translated from Spanish), "If You Can Read Spanish, Also You Can Read Nahuatl."

Facing page one is a black-and-white photograph of a middle-aged Nahuatl woman smiling broadly, wearing a long white dress and a white blouse adorned with floral designs on its short sleeves. On her head perches a large straw basket with the contents heaped high beneath a white cloth.

The book's first chapter describes the principles of Nahuatl pronunciation, with special emphasis on *tl*, which in the Nahuatl language is considered to be a single symbol, just as in Spanish *ch*, *ll*, and *rr* are considered single symbols, completely distinct from the letters *c*, *l*, and *r*.

Most of the pamphlet is composed of stories written in the Nahuatl dialect spoken by Alejandro. The stories, written by native Nahuatl speakers living in this area, are illustrated with simple line drawings. The drawing for one story shows a woman picking coffee beans while on the ground a snake lies half hidden beneath fallen coffee-bush leaves. Another shows a man in his cornfield picking corn by hand, while a dog knocks over his water jug. Another shows a woman patting out corn tortillas by hand. Throughout the book ordinary Nahuatl activities and beliefs are treated with respect. It's an extraordinary and enlightened little book, published by the Instituto Lingüistico de Verano (Summer Institute of Linguistics) in Mexico City.

The pamphlet provides several word lists, with Spanish on the left and the Nahuatl equivalents on the right. Seeing this,

Alejandro stands up and walks to where he can't see the pages and, with a huge smile, says, "You say the Nahuatl word and I'll tell you what the Spanish is." *"Tlacualistli,"* I read. Positively beaming, he answers that it means food, and so it does. *"Tlitl,"* I say; "It means fire," he replies. *"Etl,"* I say; "Beans," he laughs. We do this for quite a while.

So that you can see what Náhuatl looks like in print, here are the first sentences of a story about a man cutting a tree:

Se tonali yajqui cuajcuahuito se huehuentzi imila. Ajsiti-huetzito imila quiitzqui iacha tlen quihuicayaya, huan pejqui quitzontequi se tomahuac cuahuitl. Huan quema ya para huetzis nopa cuahuitl quitlalili se laso para quitilanas. Huan teipa quitilanqui nopa cuahuitl huan hualajqui imelac campa ya itztoya huan amo huelqui motlalo. Huajca nopa hueyi cua-huitl huetzqui ipani nopa huehuentzi huan nopano mijqui. *

*Reprinted with permission from *Si Puede Leer Español También Puede Leer Náhuatl,* México, D.F.: Instituto Lingüistico de Verano, 1985.

Porch Woman

Those last weeks in the United States I sometimes fantasized about my visit here. Always the most irrepressible thought was this: Down here, I'll find myself a woman, and I'll undo these past months of living monklike, of being mummified inside reams of typing paper. . . .

So, during my first forays into downtown Tamazunchale, I've kept my eyes open, always looking for *her:* Fortyish, intelligent looking and all woman, and maybe a little taller and thinner than most mature Mexican women.

But, walking the streets with Martha, who has become my guide, it's been as if I were peering into a hole in Mexican society. There are always plenty of females, but each, for me, is either much too young or much too old.

"Where are the women who are my age?" I finally ask Martha.

"Inside their homes looking at their babies," she replies without missing a step.

After four or five trips downtown with Martha, I have simply given up. A long time ago I learned that nothing intensifies loneliness more than looking for someone and not finding that one person. When you stop looking, the loneliness does not abate but at least usually, somehow, it becomes bearable.

This morning Martha and I are returning from across the river. We pass Hotel Tamazunchale and a little farther down the street, on a ground-level porch about three feet wide and five feet long, surrounded by a cinder-block wall a yard high, I see sitting in a chair the woman I've been looking for. She's gazing dreamily across the street. From here she looks to be half Mexican and half Anglo.

Martha and I need to pass directly in front of her. As we approach I realize that in a few moments I'll be able to turn to my left and look at her. And, simply because I am a gringo and thus may be forgiven for a little nonstandard behavior, I'll be able to stop and brew up some kind of conversation.

Martha and I duck beneath a green and red avalanche of blossoming bougainvillea blocking the sidewalk and then come up exactly in front of the woman. Debonairly I look to my left and see that she is gazing right back into my eyes. Moreover, she's leaning forward, fiddling with her shoes, in a manner that strikes me as having been contrived to display to me her marvelous breasts.

Just to keep my balance, I must avert my eyes to the other side of the street. And across the street there is a bar, at the door of which stands a very greasy-looking little man in street clothes, dark glasses, and with gold-rimmed teeth. I sense that he considers himself to be part of this thing between the woman and me. Perhaps I am wrong but experience suggests that this woman is a prostitute and the man is her pimp.

Martha trots along in front of me looking for a candy kiosk.

In a few seconds I find myself down the street, not having missed a single step.

26

Pine Jumper

T he Rio Moctezuma (Montezuma's River) runs along most of Tamazunchale's northern boundary. Upstream from the bridge and right across the river from the main part of town, there's a narrow floodplain shaded by big trees. Because of frequent flooding, people don't live on this level ground. However, in this shaded parklike area, pigs, chickens, and turkeys wander about, children play, young men hang out leaning against tree trunks while airing their stomachs through unbuttoned shirts, and on low-hanging branches women hang their washing to dry.

Right at the slope's base, people's cramped-together houses are constructed of the same unpredictable materials as those used in Colonia el Sacrificio. Some buildings rest on cinderblock foundations and have tin roofs, but others are hodgepodges of discarded planks, cardboard, bamboo stems, and rusty sheets of tin.

The family of Pancho (the husband of Paulina, who is Alejandro's eldest daughter) lives in one of the better houses beside the floodplain. Pancho's father, Don Martín, sells fruits and vegetables from a straw mat beside the bridge and serves as a kind of middleman or wholesaler between producers and buyers. For example, the other day a farmer, or *campesino*, arrived on a bus from the arid land on top of the altiplano; he brought with him a crate of *tunas*, which are edible fruits produced by certain species of cactus. Don Martín bought the tunas and the next day sent my eight-year-old guide Martha up the road to Tamán to sell them.

On this Sunday afternoon, after selling fruits and vegetables from his mat all morning, Don Martín invites me to his riverside home for an afternoon visit. When I arrive, quickly it becomes apparent that he has just one thing about which he wishes to talk:

"They've told me of your interest in plants," he begins. "Do you know that it's possible to communicate with the spirits of plants? When you do certain things, such as stay away from alcohol, drugs, and women, and prepare your mind in a certain way, you can look into a plant and then know how that plant can serve you. For years I've studied these techniques, so I'm just beginning to learn plant secrets. Already I can make certain concoctions. There was this woman up the path, all inflamed and red around her kidneys. The doctors said she needed an operation. Well, right before her operation I took her some herbs and she got over her illness the next day and never had to go to the hospital."

An extension of the tin roof on Don Martín's cinder-block house covers an area of naked ground outside the bedroom, and this area serves as the kitchen. As we talk, the señora stands there grinding chili peppers for a broth she's fixing. Don Martín sits on a bed covered with an orange bedspread adorned with delicate floral designs. The concrete floor is painted dark green. Draped on crude poles suspended beneath the tin roof, sheets of blue plastic serve as a ceiling. On the cinder-block wall behind the Don hang a large, gilded

crucifix, three calendars with gaudy religious scenes, and a color photo of the family, wrapped in plastic. On the small, rough-hewn table beside me, spread with a powder blue tablecloth, stands a splendid bouquet of red gladioluses. Next to the door, in an orange plastic net bag, hangs half a bushel of garlic.

"The lives that we humans live are so very restricted," Don Martín continues, becoming rather nervous or excited. "Earlier, man had many more senses than the five he now has. For example, there's a kind of vestigial ear here in the throat area. In the stomach region is an organ for telepathy. And here in the top of the head is a kind of eye, the pineal gland. If someone who is truly open and receptive to these teachings is properly meditating, a ray of light emanates from the pineal gland."

A table fan drones on and on, sweeping back and forth

across the hot room. Outside, a big tom turkey raises his red and blue, featherless, warty head above a tub on the kitchen floor. He looks around majestically, then bends his snaky neck over the tub's rim and gobbles up some freshly shelled garbanzo-type beans.

"These teachings were set down by Samael Aunweor of Colombia. He died just a few years ago. Well, Samael Aunweor was his 'real being' name; regular people around him knew him by his 'world name,' which was Victor Manuel Gómez. He was the 'Fifth Angel of the Apocalypse.' One of his many teachings is that when people go to sleep, their spirits — their 'astral selves' — go to another world. I didn't believe all this until one night I got up, looked down in my bed, and saw myself still lying there, asleep. Another time, coming down off the altiplano, my *compadre* and his wife were killed in a car wreck. Eight days after their deaths, when my astral self was out of this body, I met them and we talked."

Thunder from the afternoon storm rumbles through the door; along the Rio Moctezuma the tops of big trees are beginning to sway. And who would guess that this man who sells tomatoes and carrots from a mat spread at the end of a one-lane bridge could communicate with plants and "leave my body and go there into the cool elevations where pine trees grow, and in a single leap pass from the forest floor to the very top of the highest pines. Ayyyyyy . . . what a beautiful view!"

Tamazunchale and Kentucky

Each morning I have begun to walk the five or so miles between Colonia el Sacrificio and the town of Tetlama. The path atop Tepetlayo Ridge carries me about a third of a mile; the rest of the trip is on a one-lane pebble road with weeds growing between tire tracks. Though so far I haven't met a single vehicle using the road, on each walk I do meet at least twenty country people, walking singly or in small groups, carrying on their backs loads of firewood, sweet mangoes and bananas, chickens, cut flowers, rough-hewn planks, debarked poles, handmade wooden chairs—on their way to the market in Tamazunchale.

I've begun to *need* this daily escape from Colonia el Sacrificio's clamorous anarchy.

So, the road to Tetlama climbs and climbs into moist, blue-green mountains, right past fields of corn and nopal cactus and deeply shaded ravines with trees festooned with ferns, bromeliads, and ropy aroids; the road's sides are lush with weedy wildflowers being visited by clouds of butterflies. For three or four miles I don't pass a single house, for here the farmers, like most rural Europeans, live clustered in little hamlets.

When people come trotting down this path (it is mostly downhill from Tetlama), they give the impression of being both pushed forward by their burdens and ground down by them. They keep their eyes on the road right in front of them, and I think that they see only what they have to see and probably think only what has to be thought in order to take the next few steps.

Obviously these Nahuatl speakers are dazed with the pain and monotony of their journey; I also suspect that their spirits are anesthetized against the inevitable degradation of having to accept no more than a few pesos for their loads, pesos that will buy only a small number of pale tortillas—tortillas that are so light and transient and that will vanish long before one is prepared again to bundle another load of firewood, another bag of mangoes, another cargo of bananas.

Not so long ago on farms in western Kentucky we had men and women like these; I remember them. Each weighted-down Tetlama-road man I pass reminds me of my Grandfather Conrad when he worked with my father and me in the tobacco patch. My father could be a hard worker, but the army had showed him how to make the most of plausible excuses to avoid certain undesirable tasks. I worked, too, but not well, for I had seen too much TV.

But, when my Grandfather Conrad looked with his gray eyes across the fields, I sensed that he saw—even on Saturday afternoons when we could have been in town looking around—*only* row after row of tobacco needing to be hoed, to be suckered, to be topped, to be cut. In the fields, Papaw Conrad's soul and spirit hovered in a realm where an aching back, burning shoulder muscles and hands, sweat-stung eyes, heavy sunlight, and the monotony, monotony, monotony, day after day, season after season, to him were like a tedious but not really unpleasant song.

Sitting in the hot dust at the edge of the tobacco patch is a wide-mouthed, gallon-size, clear-glass jug sweating on the outside, the condensation glistening coolly in the sunlight; ice cubes clink when the jug is lifted to pour out clean, clear water. After our slurps we stand waiting to drink a second round. A whirlwind comes along awakening the dog; each of us laughs. We rub the sweat from our eyes, and then we go to work again, my grandfather being the first to walk into the field.

When Tetlama's men hear Tamazunchale's radios playing (these men live in huts without electricity), see new faces and experience the marketplace's hubbub, and maybe even splurge and buy for themselves a cold bottle of the carbonated orange drink called Esquís (Squeeze), which costs about one-fourth of the money their load of firewood brings, then, for them, I'll bet, it's like hearing ice cubes clinking inside a wet jug at the edge of a hot, dusty Kentucky tobacco patch. . . .

A Catalog
of Birds on the Road to Tetlama

With binoculars in hand I walk the road to Tetlama; below is a list of the first ten bird species I see. I place an asterisk next to those species also found in the United States so if you have a field guide to U.S. birds, you can look them up. I'm doing this because the birds here give me such pleasure, and I want to share them with you.

Right where the path on top of Tepetlayo Ridge connects with the road to Tetlama, all surrounded by abandoned fields and pastures thickly overgrown with ten-foot-tall shrubs and weeds, the morning's calm is suddenly shattered by a loud wet-finger-being-drawn-across-a-balloon noise. Instantly, in reply, a similar raucousness breaks out in the opposite field. *"Knock-it-off, knock-it-off!"* one high-pitched screech seems to say. *"Keep-it-up, keep-it-up,"* the other is countering, in a lower, Sesame-Street, bad-guy reply. I need several seconds to realize that these are bird calls.

Before long between five and ten birds are calling,

each with its own voice, and I just have to laugh. I'm amid a flock of ***Plain Chachalacas**—two-foot-long birds that to U.S. birdwatchers look like stripped-down, slimmed-up, brown wild turkeys. After several minutes of calling, three chachalacas climb into a dead tree snag about twenty yards away. Two males sport bright red throats that stand out brilliantly against their brown bodies. As I stand listening, a Nahuatl woman carrying her year-old child in a red shawl, or *rebozo*, tied across her shoulder, passes by and I hear her gently saying, "Ah, son, listen to the chachalacas singing. . . ."

Melodious Blackbirds look like common U.S. grackles, but they're wonderful whistlers; here they're abundant all along the slope. In Colonia el Sacrificio, except for roosters and turkeys, each morning they're usually the first birds to begin calling. Probably the most typical melodious blackbird call is a very loud, liquid, almost echoic, rather slurred *chuck, weecher chuck, weecher.*

Walking past a thicket of arum family vines, I hear a birdsong that during the spring in Kentucky we hear every day. It's a ***Cardinal,** the same red-bodied, black-masked, crest-headed species that's so common in the Eastern United States and part of the desert Southwest. Maybe Tamazunchale's cardinals belong to a race different from those in Kentucky, for the call I'm hearing here has a definite Mexican accent—in general it's a fast version of the song I'm accustomed to.

Twittering in the sky above the road to Tetlama are several ***Vaux's Swifts.** These look, behave, and sound very much like the Eastern United States's chimney swifts, which are absent here except during migrations.

35

Vaux's swift breeds from southeastern Alaska to Mexico's mountainous regions; it overwinters from southern Mexico to Colombia and Venezuela in South America.

The **Grayish Saltator** is shaped like and is related to our U.S. towhees. Slate brown with a rusty brown chest and a white eyebrow stripe, its most conspicuous identification feature is its white, diamond-shaped throat. As with our towhees, its call is lusty but rather monotonous and sounds something like *chip, chup chup, woid,* with the *woid* drawn out and rising in inflection.

Rufous-capped Warblers are small, fast-moving, yellowish birds with slightly canarylike songs. They look vaguely like the many kinds of warblers we have in the States, but they belong to the genus *Basileuterus,* which is not represented by a single species with us. Rufous-capped warblers have olive green backs, yellow throats, chestnut crown and cheeks, and white eyebrow stripes. Around Tamazunchale, warbler species are not nearly as well represented as they are in most of the United States, though during spring and fall many U.S. species migrate through here.

*White-collared Seedeaters range from southern Texas to Panama. They look like house sparrows, except that they're a lot smaller, their bills are much more stubby, and adult males bear a white ring around their necks. They flock in weedy patches along roadsides.

*Groove-billed Anis look like black grackles, except that their bills are of the kind that parrots have. In most U.S. field guides, both smooth-billed and groove-billed anis are illustrated. Before I saw my first groove-billed, I worried about whether I'd ever get close enough to see the grooves. I shouldn't have worried; the grooves are easy to see. Anis are closely related to cuckoos and roadrunners. The groove-billed species, very common here, is found from southern Texas to Argentina.

Yellow-faced Grassquits, closely related to our buntings, are found in brushy fields, grassy clearings, and weedy roadsides; they're warbler-size birds with thick, seedeaters' beaks. Their bodies are of a dark olive color except for the chest, which is black. The male's head is adorned with darkish orange yellow eyebrows and throat patch.

Perched quietly inside a shadow-filled tree, a **Crimson-collared Grosbeak** looks as if it is entirely black; however, the moment it flits into sunlight, its blood red underbody and stripe across the back become immediately apparent. This species is found only from southern Nuevo León, a few miles north of here, to northern Veracruz, a few miles south of here; therefore, it's especially fun to see.

The Healer from Matlapa

I'm sitting on Alejandro's porch sipping zacate limón tea when up the footpath climbs a small, slender woman of perhaps fifty-five years. Accompanying her is a boy of maybe five, carrying a large web-plastic bag packed full of other bags of assorted sizes and shapes. The woman offers each of us a typical Nahuatl handshake—a slight touch of the open hands. She apologizes for having come late.

"With the rains, the river has been so high we couldn't get across," she explains. "I come from very far, you know, from a ranch near Matlapa."

She and the boy look like a pair who sometimes pass by peddling home-baked sweet breads so I pay little further attention to them; their Spanish is very fast, mostly mumbled, and full of local slang, and I must save my brain for other chores.

But after a while the conversation becomes animated and Paulina says, "Well, we're not going to pay until we see whether you've done some good. As for an egg, I'll give you an egg right now."

Paulina enters the house's attached shed area that served as a bakery when Alejandro and his wife lived together; they also used to sell sweet breads in the streets. She returns carrying a single raw egg. With a pencil, the woman from Matlapa then scratches unintelligible marks on the egg, takes by the hand Paulina's five-year-old Nanaya, and leads her to a small chair on the porch. At this point I have to ask what's going on.

"Nanaya is sick," I'm told. "This healer has come to cure her."

"What's wrong?" I ask, thinking that I've seldom seen such a lively, healthy kid.

"The healer is going to take a fear out of her," explains Sergio, Lolín's live-in boyfriend. "A while back a tree fell near Nanaya and ever since then she's been nervous. She sleeps with her eyes open and jerks. If this fear isn't taken from her, it can develop into a bad problem. She'll go crazy and have sores. . . ."

The healer rapidly waves the egg back and forth across Nanaya's back, up and down her arms, across her chest, and up and down her legs, all the time chanting in a low voice. Then the egg is laid aside and the healer begins massaging Nanaya's right arm in a strange, vigorous manner. Nanaya smiles as if she considers the whole thing to be a lark.

"No problem now," the healer announces, apparently having felt no fear in Nanaya's arm.

"What about the powder?" asks Sergio. "Aren't you supposed to put ground-up, toasted avocado leaves here inside the elbow, and if the powder falls off, the fear is still there, but if it stays and burns, the fear is gone?"

"I don't use the powder," replies the healer, a little defensively.

Now the woman asks for a glass half filled with water and

39

empties the egg's contents into it; the yellow yolk and clear protein sink through the water to the bottom of the glass. As everyone watches, slowly the protein's upper surface—the submerged interface between the top of the protein and the bottom of the water—begins turning white. Stringy little spires of coagulated white protein rise upward through the water. An exaggerated, white alpine landscape is formed inside the water, on top of the mass of clear protein.

"That highest, white strand in the middle is the tree," the healer interprets with an air of authority. "You can see the child lying here atop this clear spot next to the tree. If I hadn't removed the fear from her, that whiteness wouldn't be forming. I've healed the child."

For a long time everyone examines the egg. Then the healer removes from one of her bags a freshly cut mint. With several fresh sprigs she brushes Nanaya's body from top to bottom. Once a strong minty odor suffuses the air around us, the healer tosses the used mint over the embankment.

"She is washed completely clean of all fear now," pronounces the healer.

"Come back on Wednesday," says Paulina. "If she's cured, you'll get your money then."

"If I don't get my money then, the girl will become very sick," counters the healer from Matlapa.

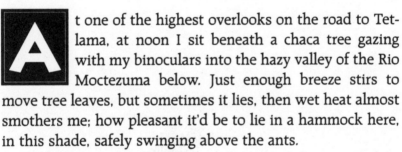

Pot of Gold

At one of the highest overlooks on the road to Tet-lama, at noon I sit beneath a chaca tree gazing with my binoculars into the hazy valley of the Rio Moctezuma below. Just enough breeze stirs to move tree leaves, but sometimes it lies, then wet heat almost smothers me; how pleasant it'd be to lie in a hammock here, in this shade, safely swinging above the ants.

Heading for Tamazunchale, a man comes along carrying a truck battery on his back, in his *ayate*. I offer a smiling buenos días and pay no further attention. But he stops to talk.

Not as shy as the others and apparently he's been around a little, he's saying that his name is Francisco Martínez and that when I pass through Tetlama I should visit him, for his home is a little beyond town where the trees are big and the animals special.

"There, the chachalacas are big as turkeys and they come right up to the hut, so you can take your pictures," he says smilingly, somehow slyly; I have said nothing about carrying a camera. "Big squirrels, completely black, everywhere, everywhere. Animals big as pigs, with a name you've never heard; we shoot them, they fall from the trees, and they taste better than pig. *Ay, qué sabrosaaaaaaaaa . . .*"

He hisses out his "*aaaaaaaa . . .*" and I sit thinking how unusual it is for a Nahuatl speaker to understand that probably I'd never have heard their local name for this creature that tastes better than pig.

"When you come, let me lead you there to that peak," he offers, pointing to the highest mountain behind me, a peak with slate gray clouds caught around it. "It doesn't look so high, but when you get up there the wind is cool and fresh and the slope becomes steeper and steeper and plants and animals live there that can be found nowhere else on earth."

His words sound generous and full of promise, but something about the moment feels off-balance. I sit feeling this so strongly that I fail to react to his words, and this seems to spur him on, to cause him to become more enthusiastic, more dramatic, and almost grotesquely ingratiating.

"There at the very top someone has left some large coins," he says with his eyes open wide. "Ah, and they are this large, *very* large, a whole pot of them, but they are coins that today no longer are used."

I recall the large, copper twenty-centavo pieces in use here fifteen years ago. Even then, when the peso was 12.5 to the dollar, those coins weren't worth much. Now that it takes 2800 pesos to make a dollar, they would be worth less than a hundredth of a U.S. cent. Thus, if I *try,* I can visualize someone hoarding them, just to sell later as scrap copper.

"Gold," he says. "The old coins are gold, and I can show you where they're found, right up there in the clouds, right now . . ."

He is standing and I am sitting. His face is turned so that it meets the sky far above and to the right of my right shoulder. So, Francisco Martínez is standing there looking at me obliquely through eyes that now are tightly slitted and profoundly Oriental. His black hair shines in the heat; his skin is dark golden brown and so wet and smooth that it looks like plastic; his cheekbones are massive and high, and behind him are small, silhouette-black *chaca* leaves quaking incongruously tranquilly in the wind; beyond that, white cumulus clouds hang in a baby blue sky; and his statement that the old coins are gold flashes into the shimmering afternoon like some kind of electric spark.

In what world or what century must be this man's mind if he thinks he can get by with talking to me like this? He's about my age. He's showed superb self-discipline in developing his tale, and his talent in exercising sincere and proper facial expressions and tone of voice has been artful.

He looks down at me and I look right back, hard into those black slits. For a long time neither of us says a word and neither blinks or looks away. It's one of those exquisite moments when East confronts West, and it's powerful and who knows how'n hell this is going to turn out?

"I have no interest in looking for gold," I say, and he smiles an "*Ahhhhhhhhh . . .*" and keeps looking at me obliquely, but now with his eyes unslitted.

Does he wish to rob me, there on a slope beneath slate gray clouds? Does he want to see if gringos are as gullible and money hungry as probably he's heard? Does he just have a wry sense of humor and want to set me up for a joke to share later with his friends? He asks for some change so he can buy whiskey in Tamazunchale.

I refuse.

He says he must go. I rise to shake his hand. And when I reach out it occurs to me to offer a solid, gringo shake instead of the timid hand touch that these Nahuatl-speakers use.

44

But, though I stand a foot taller than he, his shake also is powerful and self-confident.

"I'll see you again," he says as he walks away, straightening the ayate's strap upon his head.

Return of the Healer from Matlapa

Three days after the first visit of the healer from Matlapa, the small woman and her little boy return. Paulina agrees that Nanaya has been cured, so the fee is paid.

But now the healer claims that a further problem exists and that another, much more expensive cleansing is required. Problem is, when the tree fell beside Nanaya, somehow the girl's shadow got trapped there beneath it. Of course, it isn't the "sun-shadow" that's trapped but another kind of shadow we all have. If the girl doesn't get her shadow back, she'll have bad problems. Now the healer needs enough money to buy for a getting-the-shadow-back ritual several candles, whiskey, and two sacrificial chickens.

Paulina makes a little money each day taking in other people's clothing to wash; most nights she's unable to sleep well because of sore back muscles and chapped hands. Now I sit on the porch watching incredulously as she forks over several days' wages for a second "cleansing." And this money is not even for the souped-up, two-chicken ceremony to get the girl's shadow back but only for another mint cleansing that maybe will keep things under control until enough money can be scraped together to pay for the two-chicken ceremony.

During Nanaya's second mint cleansing I ask the healer if for the equivalent of fifty U.S. cents she'll let me take pictures. She agrees, but she won't let her face be photographed. During this second cleansing I learn that the healer is chanting Nahuatl. After the mint cleansing another egg is waved across Nanaya's body; once again the protein turns white when it's emptied into a glass of water.

When the healer leaves I do not express my feelings about what I've seen; somehow I sense that I should not attack these beliefs that during really hard times may be the only source of hope for desperate people. But I do suggest that it would be interesting to shake another egg for a bit, as if it were being waved across a body, and then drop it into water to see if the whiteness forms. Everybody laughs and no egg is sacrificed.

By the way, on this second visit, the healer brings along a package of herbs for me. If I consume these herbs, she says, any woman I want will find me irresistible.

Crash

aybe a bacillus or maybe just last night's bad dreams, but somehow I have the feeling it all started yesterday on the path atop Tepetlayo Ridge.

There a whole cloud of butterflies perched on and flitted above a green pile of pig shit, but as I walked along all I saw were generous mangoes suspended in tree limbs above—mangoes baby-head large, plum-red on top, yellow-green below, and dabbled all over with silvery glaucous bloom. So, for the first time in my life, I stepped on a negligent butterfly, leaving its brown, red, yellow, and blue wings askew in the flattened green shit.

Then last night this dream came again and again: I had two women with wondrous white breasts; little puckery wrinkles radiated through soft, lightly pigmented brown skin, away from hard, black nipples. But before I could have one woman, the other would start sliding off the bed; then I would work with her, but before I could have her, the *other* would start slipping off. Usually I can interpret other people's dreams but not my own; of this dream all I can say is that somehow I have the feeling that those women tie in with the smashed butterfly and pig shit and today's sickness.

Not gringo-three-days-in-bed-nothing-but-vomit-and-diarrhea sick, but sick nonetheless. Just lifting the typewriter from the tent leaves me sweating, trembling, and white-knuckled. One-eyed Doña Feliciano across the coffee patch right now is vomiting—the dogs are lapping it up—so maybe the Doña and I got our infirmities off the same whiff of dust.

Paulina comes to sit with me, asking why I'm so sad; I explain that I'm just sick. Then for some reason I tell her how in August in Kentucky the days stay hot, as hot as here and even hotter, but Kentucky in August has dry heat that almost feels cool in the shade. Moreover, the evenings up there are starting to cool off a little, and how nice it is in August to sleep at night next to an open window. Of course I do not tell her nor admit to myself that in this air-conditioner era few Kentuckians besides me sleep next to open windows.

Continuing my nostalgic ramblings I point out to Paulina that in Tamazunchale the cicadas are droning in trees and at night the crickets chime, just as they do in Kentucky; but all trees, shrubs, and weeds here are deep green, just as they were in June and July, while in Kentucky right now, because of the dryness and the approach of fall, a certain kind of yellowness is coming into the trees.

When Paulina leaves I lie for a long time thinking about what I'm doing here, and I must admit: This green, noisy slope has become for me that earlier rhapsodized bowl of "shimmering, oversimmered, too-spicy, and . . . slightly disreputable stew." However, now for me it's a stew going sour. But out of that rises a ray of light. That ray of light is the road to Tetlama and beyond. . . .

Therefore, I'll stay here beneath the cocuite tree until I've used up my rent and then, by God, I'll strap on the blue backpack and walk to Tetlama and then beyond and beyond, and maybe even into the higher elevations where oak and pine grow, and where it's cool and dry, and instead of Nahuatl the country people will speak . . . who knows?!

The Scorpion and the Ants

O n the road to Tetlama, beneath the noonday sun, inside weeds avalanching off the ten-foot-high, more or less vertical cliff of limestone, I hear grasshoppers thumping against stems and leaves. At the road's edge crickets, spiders, and something like silverfish stampede from the weeds onto open gravel. A cricket jumps from the grass, then jumps again and again, zigzagging upon the road crazily, stupidly; one of its antennas and a leg are missing. Then I notice a sound a little like that of a flowering plum tree full of tiny bees, except that this sound is quieter, wetter, and somehow more coldly persistent.

Focusing my eyes through the weeds onto the ground and stone below, over an area of the cliff's face about six feet wide and fifteen feet long, I see streams of medium-large black ants; the streams are five to ten ants wide and some streams flow one direction while other streams flow the other, but most of the streams are heading generally northward along the cliff's face.

I'm not sure what's making the wet bees-in-a-plum-tree

sound because these ants don't have wings. Maybe it's just those millions of black legs moving so methodically, so nervously, so irrepressibly fast. As I watch, a two-inch-long scorpion, its curved stinger held crookedly and not so confidently above its back, is flushed from a crack in the cliff's stone.

The scorpion emerges with several ants holding on to its legs with their mandibles. Heading for the antless road, several times the scorpion runs across columns of ants and at each crossing it gathers a few more ants. Finally, still not close to the road, the scorpion climbs onto a fallen, tilted weed stem and holds on silently while right beneath it a thick, fast column of ants streams by, never sensing the scorpion's presence above them.

However, there's a built-in element of randomly applied snoopiness in these ants, for while the great masses of ants go only where other ants go, from time to time certain individual ants do break away and explore just a little beyond the ever-changing perimeter of the mass or enter those areas between ant streams where they explore rock crevices or do such things as climb up fallen, tilted weed stems . . .

Probably if our scorpion had stayed perfectly still, the ant explorers would have crawled right over him without knowing it. However, seeing the ant scouts coming, the scorpion becomes unnerved and bolts away; before it reaches the road's edge, it pauses briefly on a blade of grass arching above the ground. The grass blade collapses beneath the scorpion's extra weight, dumping it right into the thick ant column streaming below it.

Instantly the scorpion becomes invisible inside a ball of thousands of legs, antennae, abdomens, thoraxes, and tiny heads with black, unblinking compound eyes. For some reason the scorpion now makes no effort to escape; maybe the physiological shock of receiving so many injections of venom into its body scrambles its nerve impulses, or maybe it just senses in its own scorpion way the futility of trying to save itself.

Like any good student of natural history, I poke a grass stem into the seething mass; instantly a column of ants comes rushing up the stem toward my fingers. I withdraw the stem and am surprised to see its poking end dripping with blackness, as if it had just been withdrawn from a pool of thick, ropy oil. This blackness consists of ants with linked-together legs; ant holding on to ant holding on to ant. . . . Ants rushing up my poking stem think that maybe the stem is their enemy; they arch their bodies so that the tips of their abdomens jab at the stem's surface and they bite the stem determinedly.

Back at Alejandro's, I begin telling Lolín my scorpion-and-ant story. Before I really get started, she interrupts:

"Ay, those are the ants that clean our house for us!" she laughs. "Just this spring, on a Sunday morning when we'd gone down to the market, when we got back we found the house swarming with them. Well, what could we do? We were glad to have them. Those ants go into every corner of a house and eat scorpions and spiders. So we just walked around visiting neighbors for a while, and when we got back the ants were gone. That happens every now and then. Once Sergio was taking a bath when they came, but he just kept throwing water on them until he could finish."

Therefore: One person's material for a horror story may turn out to be another person's *broom!*

Ant Algebra

In the afternoon when the heat, humidity, filth, and anarchy are most debilitating, I lie beneath the cocuite, too hot to sleep, too unfocused to read or write, my very spirit draining out in sweat. I struggle toward organization, toward accomplishment; except that I do not wish to lift a finger. In my mind, then, distracted only by cream-colored light filtering through half-closed eyelids, I dissect abstractions, lay the pieces here and there, and look for hidden relationships.

In this state I am haunted by images of twittering, anxious legs and antennae of army ants. Maybe it's because I recognize that yesterday I was confronted with a manner of intelligence bespeaking another kind of soul, maybe a soul thriving on currents of reality that for my own manner of being are venomous. Instead of being a seed soul struggling to assemble itself and speak coherently, it was a soul exulting in its very dispersion, in having its hectic cells run around on black legs, its hormones and nerve impulses carried around by individual, hard-bodied ants, ants blindly serving the mother-mind-abstraction-somewhere-there-flowing-beneath-the-weeds-all-dragging-in-and-eating-scorpions-crickets-grasshoppers-spiders-silverfish. . . . And that wet bees-in-a-plum-tree sound . . .

Some ant streams were flowing one way, and other streams were going other ways, but more streams were flowing one way than any other, so gradually the whole mass did flow inexorably in one direction. The individual ant either simply flowed with its sister ants or else it separated from the others and wandered apparently aimlessly in a small area within the mass, or to the mass's very edge; when an ant reached a certain invisible boundary, it stopped there as if slamming against a glass wall. And, how *efficient* and thorough was this ant-mass machine in capturing and devouring its randomly encountered prey.

It's as if the ant god had said, "Ants, I propose a trade. You do this: You individual ants give up all traits of individuality. You may go with the masses, or if you wish to march apart, I give you just so much of probing into cracks, climbing stems within the ant mass, and of going to the mass's edge, but no further. In return, I do this for you: I relieve you of all responsibility, other than that of following my orders. And, most important for you, I make sure that your bellies are never empty."

And as ant individuality *decreased* by X, ant-mass effectiveness *increased* by Y. I cannot determine whether those ants are the quintessential fascists or the ultimate communists. Could it be that ants reveal how communism and fascism, when carried to their logical extremes, are the same thing?

I lie here embedded in Colonia el Sacrificio's delirium of sound and mostly stinking odors. My back muscles ache from having just carried water from across Tepetlayo Ridge, my ankle is smeared with pig shit because I've stepped in another pile but am too lethargic to wipe it off; and now for me Colonia el Sacrificio becomes the ant-mass thing there on the limestone wall on the road to Tetlama.

Silhouettes with Flowers

t first on the road to Tetlama, here's what I thought: *These people I'm meeting, they're all the same!* Each person was small and dark, wearing patched clothes, and carrying heavy loads. I theorized a lot on how poverty had evened everyone out.

But a few days passed and then where earlier I'd seen only black hair, golden-brown skin, and high cheekbones, now I began recognizing individuals. After a whole month on the road to Tetlama, finally I'm seeing that every person I meet is as unique as the farmers and shopkeepers in the small Kentucky town to which I'll return when I go home. Here is a sample of the people I meet today, in the order in which they come:

> - Bringing down a load of firewood, a twenty-year-old man/boy with very soft and glossy black hair, long eyelashes, and soft mouth and eyes carries his firewood almost daintily. He glances at me sideways and smiles shyly.
> - Carrying an unidentifiable burden in his ayate, a

middle-aged man comes with his patched clothes exceptionally clean. He walks fast and with self-assurance. His face, though of a common sort, is handsome. He reminds me of a certain bricklayer back in Kentucky—a hard-working Republican "pillar of the community."

▪ A woman of about seventy comes in a pink, one-piece dress. Despite nearly all of her teeth being rotted out, she smiles broadly all the while she speaks. She talks almost childlike, drifting from one subject to another; she pokes fun at herself and her neighbors for being so poor, and at me for being so huge and hairy. "At the spring they told me about the big gringo who walks this road," she says. " 'Well, here's someone I've got to meet,' I said."

▪ A slender, middle-aged man passes, carrying a large bag of edible orange-yellow squash blossoms. His patched clothes are also very clean and somehow arranged upon his scarecrow frame with a certain flair. He conveys a quintessential funeral-home-director attitude. "I'll bury you very prettily for a dollar," his smile seems to say.

▪ A young man of about twenty-five, with a Ricky Ricardo face, his collection of shiny black hair too large for his little head, comes smiling. He has good teeth, sparkling eyes, and he laughs as if he's always laughing and always looking for good times. He's whistling, a rare thing among these Nahuatl speakers. Carrying nothing, he explains that he's just on his way to Tamazunchale to see some friends.

Someone in Tetlama or beyond must be a carpenter, for about every third day I meet a man carrying a handhewn, wooden casket—curved top and all—on his back. Often I meet men carrying a single, massive, rough-hewn wooden board.

Especially among older people you can see every kind of wild plant being carried to the market. A surprising number of these are touted as being medicinal herbs good for the kidneys.

Also, Tamazunchale must be a wonderful market for flower bouquets. A man or woman carrying a bag or ayate full of fruit, firewood, chickens, or who knows what in one hand will also be carrying a really beautiful bouquet, prominent among which are red roses and various colors of gladiolus. Because the colors in these bouquets always are well coordinated, it seems that someone who understands flower arranging must be sending them down. How incongruous to see gnarled old men, young women, no-nonsense middle-agers carrying firewood, little children with a hen under one arm — all coming down the road carrying these gorgeous bouquets.

This morning I'm climbing the trail where it rises steeply toward the southeast. The sun is right in my face, so to avoid being blinded I just look at my feet, watching silvery drops of sweat drip off my nose. But sometimes I must glance up the road to see where I'm going.

And here comes an old man, his dirty hair spiking in every direction. He's bow-legged, swaying back and forth beneath a heavy load of firewood, and the raggedness of his clothes shows, even though he is silhouetted with the sun exactly behind him. In his left hand he carries an especially fine bouquet.

The sky blazes blindingly behind the old man's silhouette; from the man-silhouette's hand issue leaf-and-stem silhouettes, on top of which red, yellow, and orange orbs explode full of light.

Like an angered demon the descending anonymous silhouette chastises me for having ever believed in the dull unifor-
mity of these people, but, having after so many days of meditating and walking on the road to Tetlama and at last seeing
the truth, now I am forgiven and rewarded with dancing
flower abstractions.

Whitewash

Last Saturday the owner of the plot below spent the whole morning hacking with a machete the yard-high weeds below his mango trees. In the afternoon he mixed up a bag of lime and water and white-washed the trees' trunks. He did a sloppy job, so the cut-down weeds and tattered leaves around the trunks got splattered. Several days later, however, the splashed litter has withered away, or else it's been turned over by scratching hens and rooting pigs; now the whitewashing job looks fine.

When I was a child on my parents' farm in western Kentucky, each summer my father whitewashed the trunks of the catalpas, box elders and red maples in our yard. It was our conviction that the white trunks gave the place a neater appearance and on summer's hottest days somehow made us feel cooler; maybe the fellow down slope here feels the same. A great deal about life in Colonia el Sacrificio and surrounding areas reminds me of life in Kentucky in the 1950s. Here are a couple more examples:

Alejandro's unpainted, ramshackle house can be reached only by climbing a highly eroded, forty-five-degree sloping footpath connecting the porch with the trail below the embankment. In wet weather it's almost impossible to negotiate unless you're barefoot and can dig your toes into the mud. Since I'm trying to avoid hookworms by wearing shoes, several times I've suffered bad slips. This path could be fixed in two hours of hard work, but it's just been getting worse during the ten or so years Alejandro has lived here.

Similarly, all water used by the nine people here is either rainwater collected off the tin roof into barrels (barrels working with mosquito larvae), or it's carried in buckets from the spring on the other side of Tepetlayo Ridge. It's possible to rent a plastic hose carrying water from up slope, and several of Alejandro's neighbors have done this, but Alejandro claims he can't afford it.

Despite having these two "poverty indicators" pointing at him, Alejandro has paid to have electrical wires brought in — wires that are strung dangerously low through the trees. The electricity's main use is to run a knobless TV and a radio with a shattered case. Thus Alejandro's priorities are fairly clear.

I've seen the same thing in the poorest corners of Kentucky. In the 1950s it was not uncommon to see homes with badly leaking roofs and collapsing porches sprouting expensive, long-range TV antennae. It seems that after the members of any society have their immediate needs for food and clothing taken care of, and there's some kind of roof over their heads, the next order of business becomes getting "tuned in" to the broader world. TVs, transistor radios, even wristwatches that bring us into the time reference being used by everybody else . . .

Whitewash . . . hookworms . . . transistor radios. . . . In this heat and humidity, I'm having a hard time thinking co-

62

herently. With heavy rain pounding the tent's canopy not two inches above my head, I sit with the typewritter on my crossed legs, struggling to write in a focused manner; yet constantly my mind seeks to drift, like a wandering pig rummaging in this or that garbage heap.

I tell myself that in this valley I am watching great themes on the subject of human survival being worked out, and that I must document what I see in the same loving manner that as a naturalist I have documented birds and blossoms. However, at the end of this rain-filled day it is a difficult task as I sit alone in my tent, sweating, stinking of mildew, surrounded by anarchy and mud.

Station XEGI

On top of a hill across the river, Tamazunchale's only radio station, with the call letters XEGI, operates from an old house painted dark green inside with a spacious, open veranda. Two young women with desks on the veranda receive Alejandro and me during our visit; we're invited into the announcer's cabin to chat between records.

The announcer, an effective young man smelling of aftershave, asks us to write down our names; he greets us over the air. When Alejandro and I return through town after our visit, several grinning acquaintances report having heard the greeting. XEGI's 500-watt signal is the only strong signal that can be heard during the day in Tamazunchale.

In fact, during every hour of every day, anyplace in Colonia el Sacrificio, you can hear XEGI's music—the same song from every house, sometimes loud, sometimes soft, but always there, even when the homes are hidden beneath green trees.

Being inside this valley of music can require some psychological engineering. If you're of the head that others should not impose their taste of music on you or if you're just tired of hearing loud noise or if on a certain day you're in a slow mood but XEGI keeps playing fast music, the station's unceasing *música tropical* can inflame the spirit to the point of rage.

But other times, if you can just yield and accept and flow . . . become a real member of the society of Colonia el Sacrificio . . . something rather magical happens.

Many of XEGI's songs are incredibly repetitive. In the early afternoon certain of the most repetitive pieces are played for extended periods while the announcer introduces here and there brief ads and salutations. If you listen closely during these midday long-plays you can hear from every direction children clapping and singing along. During these moments this valley's cacophony and anarchy constitute themselves into a single thing. . . . Something lying in the sun, simply rejoicing in being itself.

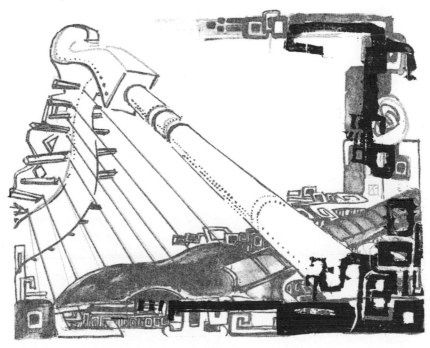

Completely uninhibitedly the valley keeps pace with the beat; absolutely unashamedly it produces nothing for commerce, nothing for posterity, nothing to be proud of. . . . It just hangs loose, feeling good, being a thousand different naked kids in a thousand different shacks dancing, clapping hands, slapping bare feet on concrete or dirt floors, not worrying about when the music will end, not remembering when it began, not caring where they are, or *what* they are at that very moment.

Fruits and Weather

ere are some general botanical and climatological observations from my past month of living beneath the cocuite tree:

At first the landscape here did not seem to change at all as the weeks passed. But now I am aware of certain once-a-year natural events that for this slope's inhabitants methodically and "officially" measure out the year's passage.

For example, when I arrived, the mango trees *(Mangifera indica)* on the slope below were abundantly hung with large, immature fruits. A week later boys with cloth bags on the ends of twenty-foot poles began harvesting those fruits for sale. At the market I began buying five-inch broad, syrupy, very sweet, messy, and absolutely delicious mangoes for five hundred pesos (twenty U.S. cents), eating one each day. After the first two weeks, unbruised, worm-free mangoes became hard to find, and their price fell to three hundred pesos. People said that heavy rains were causing worm problems. Each morning last week, on most of the few fruits still hanging on my neighbor's trees, I could see large gashes left in the night by bats. Interestingly, it looked as if the bats had torn open only those fruits that already had been damaged by bruises and worms. Today I cannot find a single fruit on my neighbor's trees. Mango season has come and gone, though in the market mangoes still can be bought, apparently being trucked in from elsewhere.

The last couple of weeks here have constituted guava season—*guayaba* in Spanish—for Alejandro's family. Guavas (genus *Psidium)* come in many shapes, sizes, and colors. The tree beside Alejandro's porch is about fifteen feet tall with reddish brown bark peeling off in large flakes, revealing a smooth, gray inner bark. The sweetish but musky-flavored fruits are greenish yellow, spherical, and about one and a quarter inches in diameter. Most days one or more members of the family climb into the tree to shake fruits onto the ground, or else they use a ten-foot pole to knock the fruits loose. At the peak of guava production the kids filled plastic bags and tried to sell them. Of course, everyone else on the slope also had guavas, so not much money was earned. Now guava season has also passed.

Concurrently with guava season, folks living at higher elevations were carrying down bags of yellow, walnut-size, rather irregularly spherical fruits called *jobos* in Spanish but in English-using books referred to as hog plums or yellow mombin fruits *(Spondias mombin)*. These grow on thirty- to sixty-foot trees that have pinnately compound leaves similar to those on walnut trees. The other day Lolín bought a bag of jobos from a Nahuatl speaker, squashed them in a dishpan, added water, strained out the pulp and seeds, threw in a little sugar, and a drink resulted that to my taste was similar to and as good as the orange soda drinks bought in stores. The drink even produced a mild carbonated effect, which I'm unable to explain. Both jobos and mangoes are in the cashew

68

family—the family in which also we find poison ivy, poison oak, and poison sumac.

The stalk of bananas beside Alejandro's porch still is green, though the fruits look a little more filled out than when I arrived. Often on the road to Tetlama I meet people carrying home-grown ripe bananas for sale. I'm always astonished at the variety of bananas that can be found. The typical banana of U.S. supermarkets is only one of several available here, and it's a minor variety, not even much favored.

The sweetest banana is a plump, two-inch-long variety with yellow skin; another midget banana has a purplish skin and a slightly sourish but pleasant taste. Alejandro's banana is about as long as a U.S. supermarket's banana, but it's much thicker, a little pulpy, and is covered with a coarse, somewhat angular peeling. These can be eaten raw, but often when cooking with a wood fire, people place bananas of this variety

in the ashes at the flame's edge to cook. The peeling chars completely black, but inside the steaming banana acquires a new, very sweet and pleasant taste. Another variety, about twice as large as a U.S. supermarket banana, usually is fried.

The weather pattern has changed since I've arrived, though I can't say whether or not this is typical. I ask people about it, but they give conflicting answers. During the first three weeks, every day the routine was this: At dawn the temperature would be about seventy degrees and the sky would be curdled with low, gray clouds, which would burn off by about 9:00 A.M. Then partly cloudy skies would prevail until two or three in the afternoon, when the temperature would have risen to about ninety degrees. Each afternoon, storms would build back toward the east—toward the Gulf—then sometime in the late afternoon or early evening the storms would hit here, often bringing very heavy rains.

But then suddenly a couple of weeks ago we had four days with no rain at all. After that brief respite it rained huge amounts, day and night, for six days. For the last two days we've had several intervals of up to four hours without rain, but still it rains most of the time, especially at night.

My clothes, shoes, tent, and some of my books are badly mildewed. An eyelid seems to be infected; my ears itch as if I have a fungal infection in them. To be honest, the continuing heat, humidity, and filth have worn me down badly. I've already mentioned my first "crash," or period of sickness; I've also had a second illness, which consisted of four days of diarrhea and cramps, but I omitted a description of that.

Really, I need to get away from here.

Part Two

WALKING INTO
THE MOUNTAINS

Tetitla

Up from Colonia el Sacrificio, onto the road to Tetlama for about the twenty-fifth time, at midday the heat heavy with humidity, the weeds beside the road more luxurious, more full of blossoms — especially of three kinds of morning glory — than ever before. Two hours later I arrive in Tetlama, but instead of turning back as always, now I keep going, passing through Tetlama, my back muscles already hurting from the backpack's load, but I'm still suffocated and sickened by the proximity of Colonia el Sacrificio, and I absolutely *need* to climb out of my souring stew. Higher and higher I climb until there in the east the Gulf lowlands lie as on a map. In half an hour the road past Tetlama ends at a weedy turnaround in the town of Tamahlcor.

A dozen men stand at the road's end, all but one on this Monday afternoon visibly drunk. I ask the sober one, who turns out to be a bit tipsy himself, where I can find the footpath to Tamán.

"I'm going to take it right now," he replies in Spanish with a thick Nahuatl accent. "You come with me."

We climb through cornfields and mostly leveled woods and whole slopes of coffee growing beneath scattered natural trees. Often our path is no wider than the width of a single naked foot; we walk upon black mud and slippery, white limestone. I slip and tumble down the slope; clawing at the dirt to stop my slide, I dig up the largest earthworm I've ever seen, a good fifteen inches long; through sweat-burned eyes I look at its glistening skin somehow feeling that I'm drunk myself. . . .

The trail divides and divides again; never could I have found the correct route without help. In late afternoon as the sun slides behind the hills toward the west we enter a hamlet of mostly thatch-roofed huts, all close-packed on mud, but here there's less filth and more ornamental flowers and shrubs than in the Colonia. I have my heart set on finding a tent site in the forest but now my new companion, who carries a large load of various store-bought items on his back, turns to me and says:

"This is our town of Tetitla. When the coffee is ripe, we men carry coffee beans to the road. Though the town is very poor and I have little to offer and my home is not comfortable, I invite you to stay the night with me. I live in my house alone."

Tetitla is a town of perhaps thirty huts but with no road, no electricity, no sewage system, no running water, and no doctor. My host's house seems to be the most substantial here, for it has a tin roof and a concrete floor. The interstices in his pole walls are daubed with a hard mixture of dried mud and straw, and in front of the house lies a large concrete patio on which later coffee beans will be spread for drying in the sun. I accept the invitation and am invited to eat.

By "living alone," my friend means to say that he has no parents, cousins, or the like in his little house, but of course

74

he does have a wife and four children. She and the children speak only Nahuatl. As the señor and I talk, the señora continually rolls out tortillas on her stone metate while a daughter pats them into round shapes. Then she heats them on a thin metal sheet—the excised top of a metal barrel—suspended over an inside wood fire. Smoke from the fire escapes between the tied-together poles that constitute the ceiling and wall next to the fireplace; these are black and stringy with years of accumulated soot.

For supper we are served tortillas, a cooked green herb called *soyo*, ground chile pepper with salt, and coffee. After supper the señor and I move our very small, handmade chairs onto the coffee bean–drying patio. The señora never stops working for a moment.

My host asks me if I'd be willing to testify before the Mexican government about Tetitla's dire need for a road. I explain that the conditions of my passport do not permit me to become involved with Mexican issues, which is a dodge. Certainly on matters like this no Mexican official would listen to a meddling gringo, so my time would just be wasted. Moreover, with my own eyes I've seen hundreds of hamlets like Tetitla, especially in the south, having a greater need for roads than here.

The señor tells me about growing coffee, and I tell him about my trip three summers ago into the Norwegian Arctic where in late June the sun never set but instead made great circles in the sky. He thinks that I am telling a fairy tale and laughs. Inside, the señora lights a candle on the wall, kneels below it, and the candlelight's soft aura outlines her rounded shoulders and head as she prays. Lightning begins flashing all around us as a storm rolls over the ridge toward the east.

A Generous Offer

While sitting on the patio we are joined by two other men. One is my host's *carnal*, his older brother, who, it is explained, has as much authority over my host as their father. The other man is my host's compadre, a sort of best friend who assumes certain responsibilities for my host's family should something happen to him; of course my host has the same responsibilities for his compadre's family.

The conversation becomes a surreal mingling of three powerful influences: The magnanimity and amiability brought on by whiskey; the poverty that shows itself in the men's faces, their tattered clothing, and their black, disfigured bare feet; and the men's devout religious beliefs. As we speak a storm continues to brew not too far from our circle of conversation.

"I offer you total use of my house," my friend says to me for the tenth or so time. "But it is not my house. It's Jesus's. He gave it to me."

"Señor Jesús," agrees the *carnal*, pointing a machete-disfigured index finger toward the sky and smiling meekly.

Sometimes the men drift into Nahuatl without knowing it. But their Nahuatl is full of Spanish words, especially numbers, so often I can figure out what's being talked about.

"I've talked with men who have gone to work there on the Other Side [in the United States]," says the compadre. "They claim that there every house has electricity and a refrigerator. Is that true?"

I admit that for the most part it is true, and then for a long time we just sit listening to the thunder.

"Everything is different there," eventually I continue. "For example, from about November to March, it can be so cold that water freezes. The trees lose their leaves, so during the cold months the forests look completely dead, but the trees put on new leaves when warm weather returns in the spring."

"God has a reason for causing one man to live here, and another to live in a place like your land," says my host in a low, pious voice. "God knows why this life among us is made so hard. It's all part of God's plan, and we should not question God's wisdom."

"Señor Jesús" repeats the *carnal,* pointing skyward and smiling.

One after another, neighbors pass by as we sit on the patio. Since we're at the hamlet's edge and the path these people take leads nowhere, I ask where they are going.

"It's simply that they are filled with admiration," it is explained. "Never in our memory has a *güero* (a blond person [though my hair is brown]) come to this town. The people pass so that they may see us talking with you. You must understand that most people here have not even been to Valles, the big town just to the north."

"What a shame!" says the *carnal,* somehow himself sounding cosmopolitan. "It's depressing, isn't it?"

"The important thing is not to travel but to be content with one's life," I reply, just to fill the air with words I'm expected to say.

"Praise God!" agrees my host.

"Señor Jesús," agrees the *carnal*, pointing skyward and smiling. It goes on like this for a long time.

Finally I learn to say *Lascamatica nitlacuaque* to the señora before I excuse myself and crawl into my tent on the patio. "Thanks for the food," I'm told it means.

The Cornfield

I n the summer of 1971, on my first trip to Mexico, I passed southward on the Pan American Highway through these very mountains. I remember how during that trip I felt such an awful indignation when I saw how these mountains' excessively steep slopes were being deforested to make way for fields of corn.

Even then erosion was bringing white limestone rocks to the soil's surface and the Rio Moctezuma ran as brown as coffee. I took photos of those mountains; I made a slide show and for years went around to schools and groups of friends, presenting a lecture, "We're Destroying our Environment." Today on one of the mountains pictured in my slides I walk into a cornfield with a man whose father cut the original trees. But I say nothing about indignation.

"In the stores they sell hybrid seed corn, but that corn doesn't do well here," says the señor. "During each harvest we choose the best ears and use the grain from those for our next season's crop. The mature corn grains are yellow, white, red, dark purple. . . ."

The corn plants here grow about ten feet tall, taller than typical U.S. corn, and the stalks are more slender. Most stalks bear no ears at all, but those that do usually have two. In each hill four or five stalks are planted together; here there's no reason for planting in straight rows. Over most of the slope white limestone rocks are very conspicuous. My host grows about two acres of corn about half a mile up slope from his house in Tetitla.

"This land belongs to the community," he explains. "However, by laws of the Agrarian Reform, only I have the right to grow corn on this plot. No other man even has the right to be here, under any circumstances."

We climb across the slope on a path so steep, narrow, and slick that I'm constantly slipping; more than once I break stalks of corn. The señor constantly machetes weeds that to my eye do more good holding the soil in place than harm competing with corn. At the edge of the cornfield grow various plants, both wild and cultivated, used for food.

For example, the *achote* is a pale green, egg-shaped, apple-size squash growing on a vine climbing six to ten feet into the corn; often, like lanterns, its fruits hang among the corn stalks at eye level. And here's a plot that looks like chives; the plant's Nahuatl name to me sounds so amorphous that I cannot write it down; I'm told that it takes the place of onions. And here, twining fifteen feet into a tree, is a wild morning-glory vine with rose-colored, long-tubed flowers two or three inches across; it's the good-tasting soyo we ate last night as a cooked herb.

"I sell none of this corn," continues my friend. "My family eats it all, and even then I must buy corn from others. The only money I make is from coffee. And those years when frost ruins the coffee, you can imagine how hard it is for us."

Even he gets out of breath climbing up and down the slope; my clothes become saturated with sweat. Several times we stop to rest on limestone rocks poking from the ground

like bones from a wasted body. We sit facing the valley, around which peaks rise into clouds ever changing in configuration. Heaped against the western slope, a dark cloud boils and thunders, generating white rain that falls into the valley in sweeping, delicate curtains. From the east, like an immense, diffuse fog of yellow pollen, sunlight energizes the valley space in front of us.

From three directions I hear men chopping at vestiges of secondary forest for firewood needed for baking tortillas, cooking beans, and brewing coffee. From Tetitla below, rising like bubbles through the valley's moisture-laden air, come turkey gobbles, rooster crowings and dog barks. I'm asked if being in an airplane is like this, and I launch into a too-complicated description of what river drainage patterns look like and how it feels to fly through a storm.

"God has a reason for making the world in this manner," my friend finally replies.

81

The Window

y tent is just large enough to hold the backpack and me. It's oval, with the sides fixed with rain flaps that can be lifted to expose side windows covered with mosquito netting. After a day of trudging up slope and down slope, through mud and over slippery stone, being alternately rained upon and suffocated by steam boiled up by neck-stinging sunlight, I find a secluded spot beside a stream and put my tent there. A storm is about to hit. The mosquitoes and black flies are bad. I am completely soaked with sweat and mud.

I take off all my clothes and slide into the tent, quickly zipping up the entrance flap behind me. Exhausted, with my eyes closed I lie on my back waiting for my body to stop tingling. Later, when I open my eyes, I'm inside a rain-repellent nylon tube, green below and white above.

All is ordered, and there are no urgent distractions such as biting ants or the need to find shelter. I feel dry and even clean (in comparison to being covered with mud and sweat all day) and sublimely calm. I roll onto my side and gaze through the mosquito netting. A cloud of blood-sucking insects swarms inches from my nose, but now they are no more relevant than if they were on TV. Here is what I see through my window:

White limestone boulders overrun with yellow-green, mostly succulent vegetation. Therefore, everything is green and white, except that here and there appear surprising, inch-broad explosions of rose-red impatiens blossoms—the same *Impatiens balsamina* grown by my mother in pots in Kentucky. Also there's the yard-high, succulent-leafed "air plant," *Kalanchoe pinnata*, a native of Africa, but now settled in here. There's the eight-foot-tall *Cnidoscolus urens* called in some books tread-softly, and in others *mala mujer* (bad woman), but named by the people here *ortega;* it bears broad, hand-shaped leaves on two-foot-long petioles. It looks soft and succulent like a papaya tree but if you brush against it, you'll get stung with nettlelike hairs.

Not far away rises a strangler fig with a buttressed trunk at least ten feet in diameter. Also I see ferns and even some orange and banana trees. Those ten-foot-long, tongue-shaped banana leaves, the bromeliads growing epiphytically on high tree limbs and, especially, the abundant, dangling vine stems cause the view through my window to look exquisitely exotic and tropical.

Somehow feeling healed from the day's mud, rain, heat, and insect stresses, I watch through my window as large, silvery raindrops begin falling in slow motion. I feel as if I'm in a magic cocoon. Magic, because this window scene triggers in me a certain psychological event: It causes an immense distortion of how I feel about where and what I am right now.

Instead of being a bug in a small nylon tube insignificantly inserted into a landscape of tall trees, ancient rocks, and rushing water, I am the person I have always been, where I always am; the screen before me is just tuned to a different channel.

Gringo Scripts

y being able to stay overnight in a house in Tetitla and to tour a cornfield was a little unusual.
Typically when I walk through isolated Indian
villages—hamlets with no roads, electricity, et
cetera—it's very different.

In such villages, when children see me coming, they usually scoop up their marbles and run away, looking over their
shoulders with fear in their eyes. Old people seeing me coming continue doing what they're doing, acting as if they don't
see me; when I speak, their return "buenos días" is spoken as
if read one word at a time from a script. Middle-aged people
either do the same, or they stare. Unsmilingly they stand in
their doorways half hidden, looking at me as if I were a
growling, three-headed cow. When I speak, once again it's the
script-read response.

Young women often run away, sometimes frantically, or
else when I pass they stiffly look the other way. Young men,
often leaning against trees airing their midsections beneath
rolled-up shirts, stare into space and say nothing as I pass.
They freeze as if participating in a "Twilight Zone" segment
in which time stands still. Several times years ago I experi-
mented by walking right through such groups without speak-

ing. They just kept staring into empty space, not saying anything. When finally I spoke, their replies were script-read.

Of course, I understand why they behave like this. They simply don't know what to do when someone as different looking as me comes walking through town. They may never have seen a human as large as me or someone wearing a backpack or a white man with a beard. I remember as a child on our isolated Kentucky farm if a traveling salesman came to the door and my father was away in the fields, my mother and I, suffocating with fear, would hide in the closet or beneath the bed.

Of course, the thing that a gringo is supposed to do in such cases is to smile and wave at everyone and stop here and there to talk with those who seem most receptive. I do this when I can. But when village after village comes along reacting the same, for me being constantly friendly and outgoing becomes an exhausting emotional burden. I find myself looking away from groups, just so I won't have to force another long-playing smile and hear those awful, mechanical buenos díases. However, what is most troubling is having to confront my own feelings.

The thing is, when day after day people run away and no one treats me as a regular person, first I feel very sad that I'm upsetting them, and then this sadness gradually changes to annoyance. The fright in these people's faces becomes for me *stupid* fright. When they run away, I see timid, unthinking rabbits.

Moreover, sometimes, when I do not struggle to see the situation in perspective (that I am a strange-looking intruder in their community, which in the past may have suffered from the visits of outsiders), when I see them running I hear a little noxious voice inside saying, "Go ahead, sneer at these rabbits; they're expecting the worst from you; go ahead and spit at them."

Raspberry-Rose Tinsel Sparkle

From Tamazunchale climbing up to Tetlama; then through Tamahlcor, Tetitla, and Santiago; then briefly back down and across the Pan American Highway at Tamán; and now up toward Agua Zarca. . . . Climbing on a road like the road to Tetlama, at long last the hot, wet, loud world I've known for a month withdrawing into a stomach-churning memory abstraction pooled somewhere there below, there toward the east . . .

Today something completely new is in the air. For over forty hours no rain has fallen at all. And I've climbed so high that at 2:00 P.M. on a day full of sunshine it's only seventy-nine degrees. Hearing wind rustling among tree leaves, I realize that for a month this fresh sound has been denied me because of the lowland trees' soft-natured leaves and by the high, breeze-daunting ridges above the Colonia. Here sweat evaporates instead of streaming down my face, back, and legs. Yes, today I'm climbing into something new, a realm more healthy than where I've been, and a place where I can find some room for breathing.

As I climb, species of plants that I've not seen in the low-

lands appear beside the path. I hear new bird calls. And seldom have I *ever* seen so many butterflies. The largest, probably a morpho, comes on iridescent, powder blue wings. As
it flies it seems to leave behind a series of blue color explosions suspended in midair. Innumerable brush-footed butterflies orbit orange-, white-, and yellow-blossomed daisy-type
flowers, and hoards of small, variously yellow and white sul-
phurs cluster beside mud puddles; plump, black grasshoppers
and huge spiders with eight-foot webs crafted of gold-colored
silk inhabit roadside weeds.

As I climb, the image of one butterfly in particular—one
individual creature—that for a moment came and took sweat
from my arm hangs in my mind. Its wings showed a pow-
dery raspberry-rose color, a hue I've seen only once in my
life, I'm sure. For a long time I've been trying to recall where

I've seen that color, for seeing it today evoked powerfully nostalgic, long-dormant feelings.

The color is from my childhood. And I believe that it was a hue seen one evening at the McLean County Fair, back when county fairs meant a lot. Closing my eyes right now, recalling that butterfly's wing color, I almost smell sawdust, buttered popcorn, and grape-flavored snowcones. . . .

There's a metal association, too. It's a metal like the sparkling aluminum-foil tinsel borders of clown hats. Yes, absolutely, once long ago some part of child-me became enchanted by something at the fair and it sparkled like tinsel and it was the exact raspberry-rosy color of the glorious butterfly that visited me today. . . .

Up, up, new weather, new plants and animals, new feelings. . . . I am climbing toward Agua Zarca, the Nahuatl village in which Alejandro spent his childhood.

Sweet Gums

Just above Agua Zarca I pass around a bend in the road and find standing on the slope around me some old friends; it's a fine stand of sweet gums. In this land where all the trees and shrubs seen so far have been species different from what we have in Kentucky, what a pleasure to find sweet gums here—one of the best-known trees of the eastern United States.

I'm used to seeing sweet gums in oak-hickory and pine forests, in hedgerows, as people's shade trees, and as one of the first tree species to become established in abandoned fields. But these sweet gums stand on a mountaintop so high that much of the time it's enshrouded in clouds. Now for a while I simply have to sit on a rock and let these sweet gums share with me images and insights of this habitat of theirs.

As in any cloud forest, even a borderline one like this, the older trees' branches are veritable gardens on which grow green heaps of fern, moss, lichen, and miscellaneous brome-liads and pepcromias. Beneath these sweet gums, fifteen-foot-tall tree ferns rise on stiff, scaly trunks; it's hard to be-lieve that they are really ferns until I see that their gigantic new fronds unfurl from coiled-up fiddleheads in the same manner as does the most fragile fern on any moist Vermont cliff. In places where the forest canopy is open, large thickets of ten-foot-tall bird-of-paradise plants (genus *Heliconia*) hold aloft their hard-to-interpret, orangish red blossoms. And the birds . . . just wait for the next list of ten birds.

I can't see sweet gums without thinking of my former ecology professor at Western Kentucky University. Dr. Joe Winstead has made a career of studying the ecology of sweet gum. Of course he always calls them by their Latin name, *Liquidambar styraciflua.*

Sweet gum is distributed from southern Connecticut to Texas, with other scattered, isolated populations found from Mexico to Nicaragua. Dr. Winstead grew sweet gums from seeds collected at various locations ranging from New Jersey to "near Tamazunchale, San Luis Potosí, Mexico." He found that, though all the plants were of the same species and his seeds were germinated under identical environmental conditions in a lab, their growing behavior—particularly their "earliest bud burst" and "latest formation of dormant buds"— was very different, depending on the seeds' origin. Mexican seedlings showed, among other things, the longest growing season.

Finding sweet gums here pleases me. When I'm in a forest where *everything* is new, I lose much of my sense of belonging there. It's like entering Disneyland where one is overwhelmed and pleased by novel forms, colors, odors, and contexts, but where the things around you do not seem to relate to "real life" at all. Yet it *is* real here.

A Catalog
of Mountain Birds

The kinds of birds found here at higher elevations remind me of Christmas candy. On
the morning before I reach Agua Zarca, here
are the first ten species I identify:

The **Fork-tailed Emerald** is a hummingbird. Though
in the eastern United States north of southern Florida
we have only one species, the ruby-throated hummingbird, my field guide for Mexican birds lists fifty-one
hummingbird species for Mexico. And most Mexican
hummers are tiny, greenish birds zipping by so fast
that their distinguishing marks are hard to see. The
following three key marks had to be seen for today's
identification: (1) its deeply forked tail; (2) its white
eye-stripe, and (3) its white throat. Other Mexican
hummers with this mix of characteristics do exist, but
they're not found in San Luis Potosí.

Shrill, screeching flocks of usually five to seven
Green Parakeets are common sights here. Distributed
from Mexico to Nicaragua, these birds are about eleven
inches long, all green, and have slender, pointed tails.

This morning's first flock lands in a large, wild fig tree loaded with marble-size fruits. Leisurely the birds waddle along horizontal branches, passing from fig to fig, often using their beaks to pull themselves around obstacles or onto higher perches. As they feast they call loudly to their companions. Anyone seeing the intensely social nature of these creatures will never want to see one kept alone in a cage, or even with caged companions.

Not only is the **White-collared Swift** twice the size of our dingy colored, twittering little U.S. species, it also flies with much slower wingbeats. A conspicuous white collar completely encircles its neck.

In *A Field Guide to Mexican Birds*, about sixty-three flycatchers are listed for Mexico; for me they're the hardest group to work with. Most are mousy-looking little birds that don't sing or do much of anything diagnostic such as bob their tails; they just perch in plain view showing hints of eye rings, hints of wing bars, hints of two-tone beaks, and hints of crests. However, there's one small, fairly distinct subgroup of flycatcher, called the kiskadeelike flycatchers. These sport bright yellow breasts, white throats and eye stripes, and dark upper parts. Trouble is, the three kis-kadeelike flycatchers are very similar to one another. Happily, however, their calls are completely different. The great kiskadee says *kis-ka-DEER;* the boat-billed flycatcher calls with a rough, rasping *rrrrrrrr!*, and the species I see today goes something like *HEE heeHEE heeHEE heeHEE;* it's the **Social Flycatcher**, sometimes known as the vermillion-crowned flycatcher.

The **Yellow-winged Tanager's** front half reminds me of a blue grosbeak whereas the rear half is reminiscent of the yellowish evening grosbeak. This species has a lavender-gray head, blackish wings with bright yellow patches, a black-spotted back, and a remainder of mostly dark, olive-gray. In the shade it looks almost black, except for the yellow wing patches, which identify it instantly.

Montezuma Oropendolas construct yard-long, bag-like nests looking like very large stockings stuffed with heavy bowling balls; usually a dozen or so such nests festoon a single tree, which is quite a sight. The oropendola itself is a handsome, grackle-size bird with a yellow-and-black tail, chestnut back and wings, and a black remainder, except for a pale cheek patch under-lined by a stroke of red and a yellow beak-tip. Its song is a liquid chortle, something like glug sounds issuing from a large jug being poured; it's a real "jungle sound."

The **Blue-crowned Motmot** makes a very low-pitched *hoo-hoo* sound, a little like certain owls. Mot-mots are famous for their tails. Mature birds strip an inch or two of the middle sections of their two long tail feathers. A motmot tail feather, then, looks normal, except that its middle part is nothing but shaft. Often I see motmots silently watching me from dense shade inside trees, with those crazy-looking tail feathers slowly swinging back and forth. Because of this tail-swinging habit, some U.S. birders call motmots "tick-tock birds." Mexico is home to six motmot species.

The **Emerald Toucanet** is a thirteen-inch-long, thick-bodied, green bird with a huge yellow-and-black beak. When it flies, it looks as if it's carrying a banana in its beak. Toucanets are closely related to the toucans seen in pet stores; often emerald toucanets make hoarse, froglike calls.

Surely the **Brown-backed Solitaire**'s call is as beautiful as any of the world's bird calls. The solitaire itself is a plain-looking little brown-and-gray bird with a conspicuous eye ring. But, its song starts out with a liquid *weenk*, and then the *weenk-weenks* start coming faster, like an old-time car starting up, until finally the song breaks off at a fast pace, accompanied by all kinds of flutelike notes. Since the bird lives in mountain valleys where sounds take on an echoic effect, its song is usually profoundly sweet and haunting.

As with the earlier-mentioned green parakeets, **White-crowned Parrots** also are incredibly loud, profoundly social birds. They're about ten inches long, with more blue in their basically green body than other parrots, a white crown and throat, and a red patch below the tail. The thing said about the green parakeets is even more true for parrots—they need to be free. . . .

Agua Zarcan Slope Weeds

On Sunday morning at 9:30, as planned, Alejandro arrives in the mountain village of his birth; he's hitchhiked on a pickup truck bringing up crates of beer. At the edge of the bustling market square he finds me reading a book about Mozart.

Immediately we head for the home of his sister, Gregoria, whom he hasn't seen for three years. We are greeted as if we'd always been there, the señora never ceasing her work of grinding softened corn kernels for making tortillas. When the man of the house arrives, Bernardo Hernández, we receive perfunctory half welcomes; I can't say whether we are simply two unwelcome guests, or if this is the Nahuatl manner of greeting.

After Bernardo, Alejandro, and I make the obligatory visit to a nearby sinkhole ("Why come to Agua Zarca if you don't visit the sinkhole?"), in the afternoon Alejandro begins pointing out various plants growing rankly on a weedy slope right outside the hut's door. As a young boy circles us accompanied by a very large, metallic green, june bug–like beetle flying tethered to a string, I take notes. Here are the plants I'm shown:

Albacor: Delicate, nonflowering herb one foot tall, with opposite leaves and a square stem, and thus probably in the mint family, though it smells like anise, which is in the parsley family. It's the only plant here being grown in a pot. Decoctions of its stem and leaves cure stomach cramps.

Café (coffee): Coffee shrubs are planted all around the house; fruits are olive-size and green. Some of the mature beans will be sold, but most will be roasted and used here. Many homes in Agua Zarca have large, flat concrete or dirt patios where coffee beans can be dried in the sun. Here we have a dirt patio.

Camote rico: A vigorously scrambling vine that looks like sweet potato vines. Alejandro says that it produces a white tuber fifteen or more inches in diameter, which can be cooked as if it were a regular white potato. Regular-size, edible, white "potatoes" also develop aboveground.

Caña morada: It's an eight-foot-tall sugarcane with purple stems. Alejandro claims that this variety grows only in the mountains. Decoctions made from its leaves are used to alleviate dysentery.

Cilantrón: A close relative of coriander, of the parsley family. Leaves of this herb are used to flavor beef stews and tamales.

Cólica: A small herb of the evening primrose family. Decoctions of its leaves are used when pains are felt around the heart.

Cordoncillo: Three species of cordoncillo (genus *Piper* of the black pepper family) grow in these parts. The leaves of this species are crushed and placed in bathwater to make the water smell fresh. Cordoncillo branches can be brushed over the body to drive away evil spirits.

Mahuite: A small herb of obscure taxonomic affinities, also used for making water smell fresh and, Alejandro assures me, for curing cancer.

Malvavisco: A small, weedy herb with orangish yellow blossoms, of the hibiscus or mallow family (genus *Sida*). Boil malvavisco's root with guava leaves for a concoction that cures diarrhea.

Pata de nene (baby's foot): A thick-stemmed, leathery-leafed member of the spurge family. The milky latex from this plant, when applied to deep wounds contaminated with foreign material, draws the foreign material to the skin's surface.

Pericón: A one-and-a-half-foot shrub with slender, flexuous stems and opposite, glandular leaves, which smell of anise. Make tea from the slender shoot tips. Rub sprigs of pericón over arms and legs to drive away fear.

Poléo: A small mint smelling like Kentucky's pennyroyal (genus *Hedeoma*), except stronger. Tie together several poléo stems, dip them in cooking beans, throw away the mint once the beans are done, and then eat spicy beans.

Toronjil: Another small mint. When used with pericón, it increases the pericón's power to drive away fear.

White cumulus clouds with slate gray bottoms cluster around the peaks above us. Accompanied by turkeys and chickens I sit in the shade of Alejandro's sister's thatch-roofed hut writing these words, still smelling the rainbow of odors, still hearing the words about driving away fear and evil spirits, and hearing Nahuatl spoken inside the hut. The cool air is moist and mountain fresh. I sit here remembering five weeks ago standing in the Greyhound bus station's parking lot in Madisonville, Kentucky, aching to escape my life up there, that life as a gringo, a fair-skinned güero.

Now I have.

The Cave

Down the slope we go through eight-foot-high coffee shrubs growing beneath *chalahuite* and San Isidro trees, through a cornfield with stalks fifteen feet tall, beneath glossy banana trees, and then down through a thicket of ant-infested vines and bird-of-paradise plants, down to where the air becomes moist and cool, and wet limestone walls rise green with ferns and mosses, to the cave entrance that's maybe eight feet high and fifteen feet wide, the cave that Alejandro has told me about so many times. Often my friend has told me about the gray mist hanging suspended at the cave's mouth; often he has told me how the cave zigzags inside the hill; but he has waited until now to tell me this:

"Before the Revolution, when only the ancients lived here, there was a village at the cave's mouth," he says with a low voice. "But when the Revolution put the road here, the ancient people went into the cave and disappeared from this land. They hid their weapons, their trumpets, their gold—all their possessions—on this ledge that runs along the cave's wall. We can't see these treasures now because they are enchanted. But, there *is* one way to see them.

"On Ash Wednesday, you must begin fasting. Take only half a tortilla a day, or something similar, and you may drink herb tea. Then after forty days of fasting, if you have fasted properly, you'll hear the ancients at the cave's mouth—hear them calling and blowing their trumpets. And then you can enter the cave, and on this ledge you'll see all their treasures. You can reach for them and pick them up and see everything about them there is to see."

As he speaks, Alejandro pantomimes holding a box and looking into it; he's turning his head this way and that, focusing his eyes into empty space. He is mesmerized by his own story.

"But the moment you turn to carry the treasures away, the cave's entrance disappears. You must replace the treasure, and then the entrance will reappear."

We climb back to the cave's entrance, the light momentarily blinding us.

"If it were not so muddy, perhaps now we could try to climb that hill over there, called La Mesa. The upper slopes there are almost vertical, but on the top there's a flat, round rock on which the ancients left clay figurines of every kind of animal that used to live in this region—tigers, deer—animals that now are gone."

Climbing back to the thatch-roof hut, the rain begins falling, and as I trudge along I wonder how it would be to live all my life in a land so filled with enchantments.

In the night I dream that I am back in Kentucky. I wander through virgin swamps with tree trunks as large as barn silos. Eventually I come upon Mammoth Cave, which is near my home, and call to people—spirits—inside the cave, begging them to tell me the way to my family's farm.

Waiting for Tortillas

Yesterday afternoon Alejandro's sister Gregoria set a fire beneath a round-bottomed pot blackened with soot. Inside the pot were corn kernels, water, and lime. When the lime-water solution began boiling, the corn grains softened and swelled to about twice their original size. Later the lime was washed out.

This morning Gregoria pours the softened corn kernels into the top funnel of a hand-operated grinder. Slowly and arduously she grinds the kernels into a semimoist, cream-colored paste called *masa*. Most of the original corn grains were dark purple, but now this masa looks almost the same as that produced from yellow or white kernels.

While Cresencio, Gregoria's eldest son, takes over the handle turning, Gregoria drops handfuls of masa onto her metate, a massive, black, three-legged affair carved out of stone, and about twenty inches long, a foot wide, and a foot high. Its flat upper surface slopes away from the señora. With a heavy, black stone the size and shape of a large, straight cucumber with one flat face, she scrapes masa into thin sheets on top of the metate. Then she pats these little sheets back and forth between her hands making them very round and of uniform thickness.

Pat, pat, pat. . . . When I step outside I hear other señoras in other kitchens making the same sound. Whenever I sleep in Indian villages, even before daybreak, as I lie in my tent, first I smell the woodsmoke, and then comes the patting.

The tortillas are baked on a thin, round, metal platter suspended over a wood fire on the homemade stove. This stove—this immense centerpiece of the kitchen—is about four feet wide and six feet long, and roughly constructed of concrete. In its middle a regular campfirelike fire is built in a depression, the sides of which hold the platter about a foot above the fire's base. Essentially it's a concrete version of a well-planned ground fire, conveniently raised to waist level on foot-thick sections of tree trunk. As Doña Gregoria works at the tortillas, I sit and look around.

The house, about twenty-five feet long and ten feet wide, has a thatched roof; the walls are constructed of slender poles, mostly the trunks of young trees. At strategic points, especially at corners, a few large nails are used, but mostly the house is held together by ropelike strips of bark from the *guinda* tree, which looks like it belongs to the elm family. (In the United States our slippery elm is noted for its fibrous bark.)

A pole partition with a door in it divides the house into a sleeping end and a kitchen end; each end has its own door to the outside. The sleeping half contains two beds built of strapped-together poles suspended above the dirt floor on logs. The mattress consists mostly of layers of burlap bags. Outside the hut, fastened onto the wall next to the beds, hangs a single sheet of roofing tin to keep the wind and rain from blowing through cracks between the poles.

Beside the beds cardboard boxes full of clothing and wadded-up, woven-plastic bags stuffed with items I can't identify lie stacked to the ceiling. Supporting a single picture frame holding six pictures of the Virgin of Guadalupe, on the partition next to the bed, hangs a foot-wide platform constructed of sticks. On the walls all around the house's interior, hanging at odd levels, are old hoe blades and machetes, gourds with unknown contents, dried armadillo shells, plastic bags of herbs . . .

Now the morning's sunlight shoots between the wall poles; as white smoke billows toward the ceiling, slender, linear rays of sunlight dance inside it; the air smells of kerosene, woodsmoke, mud, and chicken shit. Three chickens and a dog hang out beneath the grinder waiting for spilled corn and masa. Grandpa Hernández enters and we shake hands. I ask him how to say "Good morning" in Nahuatl. *"Quejéhuit,"* he says. And *"Chipano, shimosehue"* means "Come on inside and have a seat."

Now Grandpa Hernández launches into a long, rambling discussion of what Agua Zarca was like before the Revolution, before the road came, and he drifts from Spanish into Nahuatl without knowing it.

But I don't mind. For here sits a man talking with me from the deep past, his black eyes full of stars from extinct centuries. He speaks proudly and animatedly, and I study his face. Below his eyebrows rise an Indian's high, bony ridge. His nose is substantial and his very wide mouth bears thin lips. His ears are big and his crown, bearing a good crop of black hair, is curiously round.

Ah . . . I see you, old man from somewhere else, you other kind of being, you man of cornfield mud and tortillas made from dark, purple corn—all your life threatened by a thousand demons—but always healed and renewed with pungent herbs and secret words. . . .

Yes, I *see* you. . . .

Whistler

The señora presents me with a large stack of hot tortillas wrapped in a banana leaf. Now down I go, guided by Alejandro and Bernardo, for about two hours of hard walking on a narrow, muddy footpath. Down toward the Tancuilín River, we pass great trees with wide-flaring trunks and massive horizontal branches richly mantled with gardens of mosses, ferns, bromeliads, aroids, peperomias, and orchids.

Here are the legendary *mamay* and *chicozapote*, trees with sweet fruits that melt in the mouth, and *hule*, the rubber tree, all trees that I thought grew only much farther south in the rain forests of Chiapas. Alejandro is ecstatic, for at last he can show me the forests of his childhood.

"Look, this vine climbs trees (it's in the arum family) but has fruits like clusters of bananas. And this shrub here—we call it *yerba de tronchado*—it's really rare and it's one of the most medicinal of all plants. When babies are born with spina bifida, using this, the spine heals."

This is hard to believe, but I wonder why he should mention such an obscure infirmity as spina bifida. Could this be one of those plants waiting to be discovered by Western science? It's an unassuming-looking slender shrub with no flowers or fruits; I'm guessing that it's in the hemp family.

At the river we all shake hands, I wade across alone, and Alejandro and Bernardo turn back. A sandbar beneath a large tree, except for its vulnerability to flash flooding, is a perfect campsite. Well, I'll just keep my ears open for a wall of water rushing down the valley, for I've been looking for a site just like this ever since leaving Colonia el Sacrificio.

When night comes, inside my tent I lie next to the señora's pile of tortillas. The green banana leaf now emits an odor like lilac blossoms, and to my vegetarian nose the tortillas smell like fried chicken. I drift into a sleep wrapped in the sound of water rushing over rocks, dreaming of summer days as a child in Kentucky, when the whole world smelled of lilac and fried chicken, and being alive, enjoying life, was so simple.

I stay for two nights and a day, washing clothes, floating in the crystalline water, writing, looking for birds, reading about Mozart. . . . Only one man comes, whistling, at dawn and dusk, passing through on his way to chop cornfield weeds. He lives about an hour and a half away.

When finally I leave the campsite, heading upward again toward the mountains in the northwest, I think about the whistling man, for each time he passed he'd stopped to talk, and he'd seemed very content. As the mud and gravity drag at my body during the climb, I wonder at the man. I climb for over an hour.

For most of the climb, I am enshrouded in cool mists either of morning fog or low-lying clouds. Sometimes the mists part to reveal the valley below; the river looks like a belt of silver and the trees leaning over it are heavy with vines. These are majestic views, and the bird calls please me greatly. Why shouldn't the whistling man be content?

105

Many people in the United States also travel for over an hour to and from work, but instead of tranquil scenery they deal with Interstate traffic jams or the cramped society of subway or bus travel. The whistler gets his exercise while the U.S. commuter sits in his car and feels the tension of rush hour. During the hot middle of the whistler's day, he will eat a few tortillas and beans, then take a siesta beneath a tree, while his U.S. counterpart gulps down a quick, plastic meal and hurries on to close another deal.

On the other hand, Whistler's children stand a much better chance of dying from disease than do U. S. children. And tonight Whistler's bed probably will be full of fleas.

Well, I am glad that *I* am here in this cocoon of mud, sweat, and majesty.

And now I find myself whistling, too.

Storm Prayer

I climb the whole day, first on a foot trail, then on a Tetlamalike road passing through several hamlets where children and young women run like rabbits when they see me and the men ready their machetes as I pass. Then comes the modern town of Xilitla, about the size of Tamazunchale, and I pass onto a paved road, Mexico Highway 120. This highway continues into the mountains toward the west, so I follow it through Xilitla, continuing my journey upward.

At dusk, as has been the case most of the afternoon, on my left a sheer drop-off plummets hundreds of feet to the valley floor; on my right the slope rises like a wall at about sixty-five degrees to the cloud base. I climb up the wall and perhaps two hundred feet above the highway find a lime-stone rock more or less flat and horizontal on top and large enough to hold my tent for the night.

When darkness comes, a couple of storms build over the eastern lowlands. Slowly their powerful thunderings come and go, leaving me thinking that maybe on this night no rain will fall. But then around nine o'clock a few drops begin splattering on the tent; while these gradually grow heavier and more frequent, lightning starts striking inside the valley; apparently a storm is building exactly above me.

Before long the rain is falling hard, filling the valley with a general, awesome roar; my tent sags and fills with cold mist; water seeps beneath the tent's floor, for no trench could be dug in the limestone. I simply lie in growing pools of water, trembling from the cold and perhaps also from anxiety. Anxiety, for I am suspended high on a ledge, apparently right inside this storm's belly. . . .

Lightning and thunder occur almost simultaneously, the lightning being like a fist of energy hitting a glancing blow right off the rock around me. Even with my eyes closed the lightning flashes so intensely that for seconds afterward I see afterimages of light and shadow. Just when I think that finally the roar of rain could not possibly be louder, another roar comes, a little higher in pitch, and then even larger drops explode onto my tent. I feel like a caterpillar in a cocoon on the very tip of a fragile twig on the top of the tallest, most vulnerable, storm-stroked tree.

The last time I prayed fervently I was in the seventh or eighth grade playing first trumpet and marching in my first parade, at Thanksgiving, in Central City, Kentucky. I was a grossly overweight, bashful farmboy wearing the blue-and-white uniform of Sacramento High School, looking into the frigid blue sky above my shiny brass trumpet. As we began marching down Main Street, I remember my exact words as I prayed: "God, if you can just get me to that traffic light down yonder, maybe I can take it the rest of the way. . . ."

Years passed and I saw people die, no matter how much praying was done, and in college I studied the evolution of Christianity and the Bible, Taoism, astronomy, and everything else, and finally I decided that man is so insignificant in relation to the general magnificence and perfection of God and Her Universe that it is naïve for any human to pray for special favors.

"Dear God," I pray tonight, for often I still do pray— though not to ask for Divine Intervention—"right now I give thanks that the light fist shatters and the life-rain breaks from the sky, and that I, like a worm with all-feeling shiny skin lie here curled up and alive, feeling completely, some-how a tone myself, in this music you make. . . ."

Querétaro

It's another day of climbing, but today I do it entirely along the paved road extending from Xilitla into the western mountains. The land of the Nahuatl ends at Xilitla; above Xilitla, only Spanish is spoken.

I've had diarrhea and bad stomach cramps since leaving the banks of the Tancuilín River three days ago, so today the backpack is a special burden. Probably I am not fully able to appreciate the scenery around me—those blue-green, almost vertical mountain slopes rising to the base of slate gray clouds, and the narrow valleys below.

The road ascends sharply for the whole day. People tell me that forests of oak and pine lie just ahead, but so far all I see are weed trees, sweet gum, and an occasional oak. Pine may be growing on the higher slopes, but I'm too sick to unpack the binoculars from my backpack to see. Today I just put myself on automatic pilot and walk one step at a time. In this manner, I walk up slope for over twenty miles.

I walk bent over, every two or four steps a silvery drop of sweat dripping off the tip of my nose. But this is not a tedious journey. Right at my left side rises a road cut exposing white limestone rock. This rock face and the edge of the road itself are inhabited by a wondrous variety of weeds, wildflowers, and ferns. Most of the blossoms are half an inch or less in diameter, but somehow as I plod along, their perpetual occurrence below and beside me fascinates and pleases me almost in the way that, I would suppose, colored balloons suspended above a crib affect a very small child. They offer a sweet monotony and a very congenial accompaniment.

The most common and conspicuous plant is a member of the daisy family; its flowers are about half an inch wide and bear white rays and orange-yellow centers. A mint family member holds tiny, purple, dragon-head-shaped blossoms; a twining bean family vine has dark red flowers. Morning glory vines with blossoms of the purest blues and purples are especially common. A slender, yellow-flowered dandelion is odd to see on this second day of September; and what a

delight finding a single pink spike of tiny orchid blossoms rising right out of the roadside grass.

Even the grasses here display geometrically pleasing arrangements of stems, leaves, and flowers. I regret not carrying a book for fern identification, for here ferns grow lushly and invite snooping with a magnifying glass. Beautiful spiderwebs are strung among the plants, and here and there humorous-looking, plump, black grasshoppers stare up at me. I cannot explain why on this day of feeling so wretched the whole world pleases me.

At 3:00 P.M. I leave the Mexican state of San Luis Potosí and walk into the state of Querétaro. Right at the boundary sign the road levels out and species of cactus and agave I've not seen before suddenly appear. Along the road rise fences formed of walls of five- to eight-foot-tall, cylindrical organ-pipe cactus; many houses here, much in contrast to what's found in the lowlands, are built of planed wooden boards. Pines grow along the road, and for the first time I notice that in the air there's a cool, alpine odor. I feel as if in a few steps I've simply passed from one world to another. Now the Nahuatl lowlands seem very far away.

Below the little town of El Madroño lies a very beautiful valley mostly occupied by a reservoir pooled behind an earthen dam; horses graze in grass along the lake's shores. A more pleasant setting for a camp could not be envisioned. Though because of the increased possibility of being robbed I hesitate to place my tent in sight of the road, right now I'm sick and I don't care. I need to rest beside this lake and to listen to cool wind in tall trees.

The Virgin of Soriano

On my first full day in Querétaro, rain falls from dawn to dusk. But that's fine, for I wish only to lie in the tent, cocooned inside my sleeping bag. The cramps continue, but now I'm too empty to worry much about diarrhea; for three days all I've been able to keep down are animal crackers made of white wheat flour and sugar—hard medicine for a whole-grain disciple.

From time to time I peep from my "window" and see horses grazing in the rain and clouds filling the valley, coming so close to the valley floor that it's hard to believe that mountains rise all around us. Sometimes I muster enough energy to read my Mozart book.

As I was setting up my tent yesterday, on the highway across the lake, a procession of about seven pickup trucks passed by. The first truck carried a loudspeaker announcing the passage of the Virgin of Soriano, on her way to the town of Tancoyór, after visiting Agua Zarca, Querétaro (a different Agua Zarca from Alejandro's). Each pickup carried a crowd of believers, sitting on the truck's sidings. Standing in the bed of the last truck was a statue, the Virgin of Soriano. In Tancoyór believers will come from miles around to pray to this Virgin, one of thousands of such statues of the Virgin of Guadalupe. Such processions are not uncommon here. Seeing the procession caused me to start thinking about the people I've been meeting these last few weeks.

Most Mexicans consider themselves to be *mestizos*, or of mixed Spanish and Indian blood. In the larger cities and along the coasts, certainly you can see plenty of people with European features, but if somehow you could test all those Mexicans who consider themselves to be mestizo, I'll bet that most of them would have 95 percent or better Indian blood.

Though officially the Mexican government conducts programs to encourage Mexico's Indians to be proud of their heritage, in general being *indio* is to be considered second class. Alejandro's family is 100 percent Náhuatl, but they all consider themselves to be mestizo. In Agua Zarca, the children of Alejandro's sister are not spoken to in Nahuatl; in a few years they will have forgotten most of what they've learned from Grandpa Hernández and will consider themselves to be mestizos. Being ignorant of their parents' language will in a certain manner be a badge of pride to them.

In this land populated by Native Americans eating native American corn tortillas and beans, what a wonder that we should be speaking European Spanish and seeing a procession passing reverently, carrying a symbol of European religion in a pickup truck.

The Catholic religion and the Spanish language. . . . In Spain five hundred years ago there arose a certain circumstance, almost a state of mind, that issued forth impulses carried in the bodies and souls of conquistadores, missionaries, settlers, traders, who in the Americas planted at least those two things—their religion and their language.

Since today I have in mind the life of Mozart, as I lie in my

114

wet tent I begin seeing that if a nation sends abroad such ideas as religion and language, it's rather like a human bequeathing to posterity certain melodies and the frames of mind those melodies cause, and the acts those moods inspire.

Thinking this, I hum the first bars of Mozart's *Clarinet Quintet* and I am empowered to write these very words. Are these words I'm writing and the procession of the Virgin of Soriano the same thing?

And, yesterday, that sweet, day-long monotony of purple morning glories, dragon-head-blossomed mint, and unexpected orchid . . . are they not God-tones, like the procession of pilgrims sitting in pickup trucks, like notes written in the manuscript of a man who could not stop writing music?

A Wetback's Story

"Eleven of us went, five from here and six from Xililta, all together in a bus. It was my first time. So twenty miles from the border the bus stops and a Mexican policeman gets on. 'All of you with papers raise your hands,' he said, and some raised their hands but most of us didn't. We who were crossing illegally had to get off the bus and pay the policeman between fifty and two hundred pesos before he'd let us get back on. To us, who had nothing, that was money!

"In Nuevo Laredo we all went together and hired two taxis to carry us to a certain place on the river where it was known that people like us could cross. At the river another Mexican policeman came along and before he'd let us go across each of us had to pay him another two hundred pesos. Then we had to hire a boat to carry us across, three at a time, for one thousand pesos a trip. When we all got over, the boatman said, 'Now, you all hide in these bushes until dark, because the gringos use airplanes to watch this area, and they'll nab you.' So we hid real good, my buddy under the limb of one side of a bush and me under the other. In the afternoon I saw a man coming with a high-powered shotgun. 'Don't worry,' my friend said, 'he's just a gringo hunting rabbits.' 'But he's wearing a mask,' I said.

"The man spotted us and pointed the gun at us and started cursing. He made ten of us out of the eleven go to a house where two other masked men were waiting, and they took everything we had—our money, even our food. Man, I'll never forget the feeling of that shotgun's barrel jammed up against the back of my head. So they let us go and we started running north through the desert, not even caring now if the airplanes should see us. We traveled all night and rested the next day, and so it went for three days, us eating cactus— and that cactus up there is all spines, you know. It rained at night and we were cold. I didn't even have a pair of sandals back then. Then one afternoon I was looking for cactus to eat and behind a bush I saw a man with a gun. He was with

the U.S. Border Patrol. They took us all and held us for ten hours in the Laredo jail, then sent us back across the river. Later visits I made to the U.S. also were hard, but then I had better luck. A year ago I returned to Mexico after working for a man for three years in Freer, Texas. That man always treated me very well, but he died."

This is the story of José Heraclio Mata Trejo, who early yesterday morning came through the pouring rain to my tent beside the lake. Having heard from the local boys that I was so sick that I could not eat, he brought with him a thermos of hot coffee, a sweet roll, a *terramicina* capsule, and an invitation to move onto the dry wooden floor of his unfinished store next to the highway.

I accepted the invitation, gladly, for on the third day the rain has increased and the lake now floods what earlier was the lovely grassy camping area. The temperature does not rise above sixty-two. When in the evening of the third day José brings me a spicy bean tamale cooked in a corn husk and neatly tied with corn-shuck fibers, I am able to eat it while I listen to his story.

Pig in the Rain

With the road above El Madroño washed out after five days and nights of hard rain, and the whole town without electricity because of a fallen pine, I stand at the door of the half-finished store watching the rain come down. Today I'm heading farther up the road, rain or no rain. The temperature has dropped to fifty-five so surely that signals the approach of cool, dry weather. Before strapping on my backpack, I notice a pig standing beside the highway in front of the store.

The pig has been rooting in the grass, but right now it's just standing with its legs spraddled, looking up into the sky, sniffing. A large mat of red dirt and uprooted grass lie on top of its snout, so that it must see the sky through a blurred network of disorganized grass stems and leaves. The pig's inch-long, reddish brown hair, looking like filthy bristles of a hairbrush used for a very long time without being cleaned, is matted with gummy dirt and miscellaneous dark debris; silvery globes of water hang suspended among the bristles. Maybe I have never seen a creature so thoroughly enmeshed in what it's doing.

Even I smell the morning's mud, hot tortillas, beans and coffee, human and chicken and pig manures, wet sawdust from the mill up the road, lingering diesel fumes from the last bus that passed by, and a certain sweet-mint odor that always I smell in high mountains, whether in the Alps, the Andes, or the Rockies. What must that pig smell, there in the rain?

The toilets here are built so that wandering pigs may easily pass beneath the seat-holes and eat what's been deposited there by humans. Seeing this, and then later eating those same pigs, El Madroño's children must early acquire a certain profound and practical insight into such fundamental elements of ecology as nutrient cycling, energy flow through the ecosystem, and predator-prey relationships. Who knows how the pig's sense of reality is affected by its daily perspective there beneath those holes?

Today I feel like a pig—a pig that roots superficially into whatever comes along, digests what it can, then moves along. For the truth is that today I am leaving El Madroño not because I really sense that the rain is about to end—it's already intensified since dawn—but because something about the friendliness, generosity, and loveliness of this town's people unnerves me.

Since establishing myself in this unfinished store beside the highway I have received an unending train of invitations to coffee, and hardly ever have I been without someone to talk to. Perhaps because of their poverty and life of struggle, everyone I meet, even the children, has a sharply developed personality, with all the good and bad aspects and every emotion out where it can be seen. We gringos are bland and homogeneous by comparison.

I should be writing about this wide-spreading bouquet of people, but instead I write about a pig; I should be human enough that now I would need to stay longer, but, instead, I leave now, like the pig in the rain, who—when he sees me watching him—abruptly ambles away.

The Cathedral at Landa de Matamoros

s I leave El Madroño, several boys and men point to the heavy darkness rising in the east and invite me to stay longer. But already I've said my good-byes and in me now is the need to escape.

Soon I'm soaked, and the downpour is general. After two hours I cut into the pine forest, where in the rain I put up the tent. It's so cold that steam rises from my pee. All night I am cold and wet, but the next morning, for the first time in six days, the rain has stopped.

I keep heading westward and soon the road dips. Instantly pines disappear, junipers begin to dominate, and finally as the road continues to plummet I find myself passing through nothing but head-high, scrubby oak. A limestone road cut rises on my left and the valley lies far below on my right. Half a day of descending brings me to the valley floor, occupied by dispersed little villages, scattered farmhouses (around Tamazunchale, farmers lived together, European-style), weedy pastures, cornfields, and lots of low scrub, dominated by the eight-foot-tall, spiny tree called *huisache*, or *Acacia farnesiana*.

Often in front of houses I see cars with Texas and Florida license plates. At six different stores and *puestocitos* (kiosks and corners of people's houses where soft drinks, beer, and crackers are sold), I stop for rest, information, and bottles of mineral water, for I can't find public water sources here. At every stop I meet one or more lounging men who regularly work in the United States, either legally or illegally. *Everyone* I meet has an important contact in the States.

My impression is that if the men of this area could not work for weeks or months each year in the United States, this region's economy would collapse. Certainly the little cornfields and scrawny cattle I see cannot support the valley's dozens of hamlets, each with a fair number of prosperous-looking homes. Often I see young men wearing designer jeans and carrying boom boxes with silvery dials and digital readouts. But also I see a great deal of poverty. Poverty among the isolated Nahuatl speakers could still be a dignified thing; here it just stinks, and looking at it fills one with tedium.

In the town of Landa de Matamoros, with maybe 2,500 people, a cathedral rises five times higher than any other building in town. Its elegant bell tower and orange-pink façade full of niches with life-size saints and angels create a presence dominating the whole valley. For five miles Highway 120 shoots straight at the cathedral, only to veer away at the last moment. As I walk down Highway 120, before me the cathedral hangs suspended against the scrubby valley slope behind it like a glowing angel in a green sky.

The streets of Landa de Matamoros are eerily quiet and deserted. Its few stores are among the poorest I've seen. I must beg drinking water from a private home, and what I get looks oily and disreputable.

In Landa de Matamoros I feel some kind of a vacuum. Old women enter the cathedral to pray. I suspect, as much from

123

interminable boredom and loneliness as from desperate need for divine intervention in their lives. I stand in the cathedral's walled-in courtyard, and the saints in their niches somehow annoy me with their seeming smugness. I do not enter the church, where I know there to be candles flickering in the darkness before the statue of the Virgin of Guadalupe.

West of town the highway rises into the Sierra de Jalpán. I climb to a peak and farther to the west see nothing but head-high, cattle-chewed, spiny, growing-close-together, ant-infested scrub in which it's almost impossible to find a decent tent site. Here, just over the hill from the cathedral at Landa de Matamoros, finally, I begin feeling that I have walked far enough toward the west. I am forty-five air miles west of Tamazunchale; who knows how far that would be in walking miles?

Dry Rattle

At the break of dawn I descend to Landa de Matamoros, beg some water for my canteens, and flag down a bus heading back east.

First-class bus service in Mexico is good, dependable, and cheap. Our air-conditioned long-distance U.S. buses have sealed windows so you must breathe recycled cigarette smoke. In Mexico you can open the windows and even hang from them if you wish. Mexican buses smell of strong industrial disinfectant and the bus driver's aftershave. Sometimes the windows are tinted pink or some other rosy color; often the windshield is adorned with dangling bangles, gyrating hula dolls, and Virgin of Guadalupe stickers.

Breezing back up slope I gawk from the window at little stores and ramshackle roadside kiosks where earlier I rested, dog-tired and very thirsty. Up and up we go, the diesel engine's explosions ricocheting off the limestone road cut to our right; twice we must slow down for cows on the road, and once because a herd of eight half-wild horses galloped down the highway's center.

At the top it's so chilly that we close our windows; outside, tall pines, oaks, and junipers replace the low scrub. I'm let out at the entrance to the road to Tres Lagunas. I'm glad to be back in cool pine country, and this time the sun is shining. The road to Tres Lagunas is like the road to Tetlama, so immediately I feel at home. I wave good-bye to the bus and begin walking, climbing steeply.

By noon I must have climbed to at least 9,000 feet; the temperature is only 70 degrees. The air feels crisp and moist, and in the shadows the humus smells icy, though there's been no ice here for a long time. Against a dark blue sky, green oak leaves and branches of juniper and pine all look black. Greenness here shows only on leaf edges and inside leaf curls, where usually sunlight shows up as white glare. Sounds are muffled and a certain tension lies in the air. These are tricks of high elevation's thin air. There's no better backpacking than through landscape like this.

A little after noon I cut into the forest to set up camp. The last few days have been hard ones, so I'll just do some extra reading today. White limestone rocks jut from the gummy black soil. I'm just about to sit on one of those rocks when I hear a fairly loud, dry rattle. Lately I've been seeing and hearing so many different kinds of large, gaudy grasshoppers that I assume this sound is coming from one of them. I almost ignore it, but it's so loud and persistent that finally I do deign to take a look. And there about a yard from my naked leg a rattlesnake is coiling for a strike.

It's two and a half feet long, with five or six rings on its tail. Apparently it's cold because it moves very slowly. When I freeze, it immediately stops coiling and slips beneath a nearby rock. It's the first live snake I've seen this trip, and I'm surprised to find it at such a high elevation. Its skin pattern is almost obscured by heavy, black pigmentation; this blackness—this extreme melanism—helps it to absorb radiant energy from sunlight. I'm guessing that it's a high-elevation race of the black-tailed rattlesnake, *Crotalus molossus*, which ranges from Arizona and central Texas to central Mexico.

Continuing up slope, I find that the rattler's appearance has sensitized me to all snakelike things. A grasshopper's sudden stridulations, which earlier I would have ignored, now cause me to freeze and shudder. Every fallen pine twig with rough, scalelike bark at first glance seems to be a blackish, scaly snake. My bare legs tingle with anticipation.

In being reminded so vividly that we humans must habitually see only what is important and relevant to us—that some part of our brain must block out what it judges to be irrelevant—I begin wondering what it would feel like to be really aware of *all* things around me—to be *rattlesnake aware*—of every leaf, boulder, bird, human, cloud, and gust of air. . . .

Health Officer for Landa Municipality

This blue, high-elevation numbness with blackish, icy sunshine and far-away-sounding wind-in-pine-tops is pure, immutable, geometrical, and by nature cold; it has me crystallized inside it. Mexico's "shimmering, oversimmered, too-spicy stew" resides in another galaxy far below, there beneath the eastern horizon. It's a place I've left behind, climbed out of . . .

But now here comes another whistler. On the gravel road it's a young man wearing wraparound sunglasses, bell-bottomed trousers, shirt open across the chest, and a small knapsack with a picture of Snoopy on it.

"I'm on my way to Tres Lagunas," he says with a vacuum-cleaner-salesman smile and handshake. "I'm the government health officer for the District of Landa. I go to all the little towns and talk with parents about nutrition and general hygiene. Mother's milk is better than powdered milk, wash your hands, boil your water, stuff like that."

For an instant "mother's milk" and visions of women's breasts invade my frigid blue isolation and the pit of my stomach reminds me that I am a man with appetites.

"Ah, it's bad in some of these places," he continues, seating himself on a white limestone rock beside me. "Country laborers make twenty-five hundred, maybe thirty-five hundred pesos a day, and they work from dawn to dusk, six or seven days a week. So let's say that the man makes eighteen thousand pesos a week. Well, enough beans to last a medium-size family for one week costs about forty-two hundred pesos; tortillas cost about another five thousand; milk for the baby costs about ten thousand; coffee costs two thousand; usually somebody is sick so that takes maybe ten thousand more. So what's left for shoes, clothing, and maybe a little surprise for the kids? Parents keep their children home from school and work them in the fields. Well, maybe they have to do that, but if the kids don't go to school, how will they learn about germs?"

To disinter myself from this blueness, which now I sense to be unhealthy loneliness more than anything, I tell the health officer about the healer from Matlapa and her eggs and mint.

"But maybe all that is changing," he says with a Bert Parks smile. "The political party that always has ruled Mexico, the PRI, is losing its grip on the country. There's this man called Cuauhtémoc Cárdenas."

I know about Cuauhtémoc Cárdenas. He's the son of one of Mexico's most revered political icons, full of ideas about land redistribution in favor of the poor and a more humane socialism for all. His campaign posters, in contrast to the glossy, full-color, unctuous ads promoting the PRI's candidate, either bear no picture at all or else carry a rough, black-and-white photo of a face full of anguish and indignation; he looks like a thin-necked, hungry, old-time college professor with something important and beautiful to say but who is having a hard time getting through to his students. I cannot

130

tell whether this man is simply a consummate politician with a knack for manipulating the masses or whether he is the real thing, the saint with the Truth, the man on a white horse. I do sense that he has the power to remind the millions of their misery, and to channel the resulting anger into some kind of awful force.

"But who can tell?" the health officer continues with a broad smile. "Mexico is unpredictable. Maybe things will just go on being the same."

A Catalog
of Oak and Pine Birds

At daybreak among the highest peaks the temperature hovers at forty-three degrees. The valley below is still dark, but up here orange-tinted sunlight floods in at a low angle, cutting between fog and clouds heaped against eastern peaks. Birds here are not weed birds used to steamy plantations and roadsides, nor are they exotic mountain-slope parrots, toucanets, and motmots; rather they are creatures of a somehow more ethereal nature — lighter, faster — beings at home in thin air and icy sunlight.

Curiously, the first three species seen here are birds I know from Kentucky. The **Black and White Warbler** is a breeding summer visitor in deciduous woods throughout the eastern United States; now it migrates here for overwintering. The **Black-throated Green Warbler** breeds mostly in southern Canada and the northern states but is abundant in Kentucky during migrations; like the black and white warbler, it overwinters in Mexico. The **White-breasted Nuthatch**, looking like a little penguin closely inspecting tree trunks and often hanging upside down, is a permanent resident in most of the United States and Mexico. The presence of these familiar species here affirms that tropical high-elevation areas hold many affinities with low elevations much farther to the north.

The **Painted Redstart** looks and acts like the American redstart found in most of the United States and Canada, but instead of sporting orange or yellow tail spots and wing patches, its patches are white, and its chest is lipstick red.

The most noisy and nosy bird in this forest is the **Mexican Jay**. Dull blue above and light gray below, with a kind of black mask, it lacks the crest of our blue jay and Steller's jay. Mexican jays fly about all day asking *Wink? Wink? Wink?*; sometimes as they fly they make a curious sound like fingers thumping rapidly and lightly on a wet drumhead.

Rivoli's Hummingbird, in contrast to most other Mexican hummers, is easy to identify simply because it's so large. With a length of five inches, compared to three inches for the ruby-throated hummingbird found in the United States, Rivoli's is so large that instead of *zipping* from flower to flower, it darts, almost like a regular bird. Other than its size, its two main identification features are its green throat and black chest. There's at least one other species of smaller hummer here, but it's so fast that I've been unable to identify it.

The bird book mentions two species of flycatcher with conspicuous crests and bright, cinnamon-brown underparts. One of those species doesn't occur in Querétaro, so we're left with the **Tufted Flycatcher**.

Gray Silky-Flycatchers aren't closely related to regular flycatchers; they're silky-flycatchers of the Waxwing family. These birds are small, slim, crested birds, in the United States most closely related to the phainopepla, an uncommon bird of the desert Southwest. As I walk along the road I hear gray silky-flycatchers calling *chelp chelp, chelp chelp, chelp, chelp* so constantly that I can't decide whether this whole mountain is inhabited by them or whether a single large flock is following me.

The **Spot-crowned Woodcreeper** belongs to a family of birds not represented even by a single species in the United States. Nonetheless, if you take the brown creeper, enlarge it from four and three-quarters inches to eight inches in length and splash some rusty red onto it, you'll have a woodcreeper, both in appearance and tree-trunk-climbing behavior. Mexico is home to a dozen woodcreeper species; the spot-crowned one specializes in oak-pine highlands and ranges from Mexico to Bolivia.

Finally, trogons are stubby-looking birds with long, square-tipped tails. They're forest-loving creatures that sit unmoving, giving rather mellow, repetitive calls. The one seen here is the **Mountain Trogon**, which calls *cowh, cowh, cowh, cowh, cowh. . . .* In trogon identification, the tail's *underside* is the main thing. Spotting a trogon, you need to memorize the tail's black-and-white underside pattern and then notice whether the bird's chest is red or yellow. These two features in themselves are enough for solid trogon identifications.

Part Three

TAMAZUNCHALE, AGAIN

Tamazunchale—A New Head

I return to Tamazunchale just in time for a good rain. Translucent raindrops like shining silver dollars fall in slow motion between the blue-green slope across the valley and me. Now standing on the wall beside the toilet, I tell Alejandro about the rattlesnake seen in Querétaro. He replies:

"You know, they say that there's a special thing you can do with a rattlesnake's rattle. When you find a rattlesnake, step lightly on its head, so that you don't hurt it, and then reach down with your knife and cut off its rattles. Then find a coyote, kill it, and take from the front of its face that part of the fur that includes the forehead and the area between the eyes, and do the same with a fox. These animals have the sign of the cross between their eyes, you see, and it's said that they have the devil within them. Then you put these skins into your pocket, along with the rattlesnake's rattle, and as long as the rattlesnake you got the rattles from still lives, you'll have special powers. If you see your enemy down the road just stand and look at him and reach into your pocket and rub those skins. You can take your enemy to the jail, the *federales* will open up a cell, you rub those skins again, your enemy enters, and nobody ever hears from him again. . . ."

Paulina's family, including Martha, Nanaya, and the baby, now live in a tiny thatched-roof hut along the Rio Moctezuma. Therefore, while they now worry about the river flooding (already water has stood four feet inside their hut, carrying away most of their clothing), I rent their former home.

It's Alejandro's "outside kitchen," an appendage of his house consisting of a tin roof held up by poles; it offers three cement-block walls that don't reach the roof, an open fourth side, a concrete floor, and an elephant-size, old-fashioned beehive-shaped, concrete oven used by Alejandro and his wife when they lived together and baked bread for sale in the streets. Now I even have a table and a chair and a lightbulb hanging from a pole. I am simply too weak, because of

my recent diarrhea and extended inability to eat, to go back beneath the cocuite tree.

And now I find that Alejandro's rattlesnake story does not please me the way that such stories used to.

For days I've wandered there in the Querétaro high-elevation pine-tree blueness, being something like a shadow, metamorphosing, somehow becoming weakness-wisened, so that now quaint anecdotes no longer satisfy. Rather they speak to my inability to define the deeper stream of things in this Tamazunchale, this steamy land of timid Nahuatl speakers.

Now I wish for this book to change. Now my mind must fulfill the promise of those hints-of-insights wrought there beneath Querétaro's blue pines, in the black sunshine. Now my routines must enlarge, even into the night, and now I ache to transmit significant messages—like a plump Agua Zarcan spider thumping its golden web.

An Experiment

t 4:35 in the afternoon the sky is overcast and the temperature is eighty-five degrees. Colonia el Sacrificio lies below Alejandro's shack, half asleep, like a chicken with its head under its wing. . . .

Where is the thing of substance here, about which I ache to write? If I am an Agua Zarcan spider on a golden web, then just what is my prey?

I've decided on an experiment. Twenty-one-year-old Lolín sits on the porch reading a pulpy, cartoonized romance novel; I cannot imagine anyone more at home on this slope than she. I'll simply ask her what's going on around us, tape her response, and then closely study exactly what she says; maybe in her words I'll find traces of an unexpected thought that will lead me somewhere, or maybe I'll discover that with her other kind of mind she's actually seeing something that so far I've missed. Here's what happens:

ME: Lolín, what do you see right now?
LOLÍN: *Arboles de mango, el flamboyán, plátanos . . .*

las nubes, el cielo azul. Veo una casa blanca allá en el centro. Puedo ver el centro. Veo a una señora allá bañando con un bote de agua. Una chamaquita está en la doctrina. Allá veo una casa, afuera está una niña con una falda azul. Veo la antena allá en frente. Veo a la abuelita que está allá.

[Mango trees, the royal poinciana, banana trees . . . clouds, the blue sky. I see a white house there downtown. I can see downtown. I see a lady over there bathing with a bottle of water. A little girl is studying her catechism. Over there I see a house, outside of which is a girl with a blue dress. I see the antenna in front. I see the old lady that's over there.]

ME: What do you hear right now?

LOLÍN: *La música tropical. Música tropical. Oigo que pita el carro. Oigo el zumbido de los carros. Oigo que habla por allá, que grita. Oigo a un niño que está llorando. Perros que ladran. Prendieron la tele, oigo la tele. Oigo a los lagartijos que andan arriba de la lámina.*

[Tropical music. Tropical music. I hear a car blowing its horn. I hear the sound of cars. I hear somebody over there talking, shouting. I hear a boy crying. Dogs barking. Somebody has turned on a TV, I hear the TV. I hear lizards walking above on the tin roof.]

ME: What do you smell right now?

LOLÍN: *Nada. No huelo nada, yo.*

[Nothing. Me, I don't smell anything.]

The experiment was a success, for now I feel foolish for having used such a gimmick in my quest for a theme or issue about which I could "transmit significant messages."

I'll go ahead and include Lolín's original Spanish replies

141

just to remind myself and you that though this book is in English, the world from which all these words are springing is a musical, Spanish-speaking one. Also, the Spanish language is quite nice. Maybe some of you will smile reading that a *"chamaquita está en la doctrina."*

Paper Dancing Bull

A t dusk on September 15, the eve of Mexican Independence Day, a big crowd gathers in the park across from El Palacio, Tamazunchale's "county courthouse."

The individuals in this gathering aren't standing around posturing and chatting like gringos; rather they've joined into three-shoulder-wide streams of people that flow around and through the park, doing the thing called *paseando*, which is something much more vigorous and communal than mere American "strolling"; I enter a stream and flow with them.

At six feet, three inches tall, in this crowd I am the tallest person, towering far above the average plane of black hair. With my whiteness and relatively inexpressive exterior, I think that I must seem to everyone here to be a kind of designated observer, someone sent into the crowd to see and be seen, a great pale eyeball placidly shimmering, carried by the general flow beneath trees, past shoeshine stands and boiled-ears-of-corn vendors and Indians selling corn paste boiled in neat wrappings of corn shuck (a dish called *chámil*), little wooden kiosks selling transistor radios and red, yellow, and blue plastic jugs. As I go *paseando* I'm jostled by hordes of kids wearing handsome, expensive-looking costumes that later tonight will be worn as they perform traditional dances on the roughly hewn, forty-foot open stage that just today they've set up in front of the palacio. Carried in my stream beneath El Palacio's front balconies I gaze upward into hundreds of red, white, and green lights, then float alongside the stage itself, where young men with serious expressions on their faces test microphones and adjust lighting; young Indian children floating around me seem to be in rapture.

Flowing, easing along, all alone in the crowd, being seen, searching, at moments feeling like a gorgeous Agua Zarcan spider with its golden web, I cannot precisely define what consequential thing is happening here.

Once I tire of walking, I sit in the park and meet a good woman, a teacher among the Nahuatl. We talk for a long time, but she's here only between buses, on her way home to Morelia. The town's English teacher, an announcer on XEGI, introduces himself and buys me a drink.

Then begin the dances, a poem is read by a chubby boy who pokes his finger into the night air, the band isn't so hot but the director beams so proudly that it's okay; around the big stage there's a sea of straw hats. Here and there stand middle-aged city women looking bored; the Indians, with bags on their shoulders, watch reverently.

When the fireworks begin, they're not methodically displayed multicolored fountains of gringo-kind-of-light shown high above the city but rather rockets that spew to just above the royal poincianas and earsplittingly detonate, and fire-spitting wheels that gyrate on poles tied in trees, and eight-foot-tall, long sparkling-and-popping Tinker Toy–like structures of tied-together bamboo poles with fireworks mounted on them, which keep spewing light and popping, while on El

Palacio's eight balconies spinning wheels all at once begin discharging bright sparks, and now comes a huge, splendidly white, paper dancing bull with sparklers and exploding fire-crackers carried fulminating on the shoulders of a man who is playfully chasing the screaming crowd, and then a wildly spinning yard-high fire wheel rushes through the crowd right past me at head level, guided by a thirty-yard hemp string I've been wondering about, and then to El Palacio's right a ten-foot-high exploding wall of sparkling fire in red, white, and green spells out the words VIVA DON MIGUEL HILDAGO and then another fire wall down by the cathedral cries VIVA MEXICO, and the crowd roars and a local politician leads us all in a long litany of *vivas:* "*¡Viva México independiente!*" "¡Viva!" "*¡Viva Tamazunchale!*" "¡Viva!"

And I am standing wondering if here inside this theater of gunpowder, smoke, and odors of alcohol and cigarettes and sweat-soaked straw hats and perfume and boiled corn and fried chicken somewhere there moves a deeper stream; in this patriotic music, cymbals crashing, trumpets blaring, rockets exploding, and faces raised glowingly toward the night sky full of bats, might somewhere *here* move my deeper stream? These proud parent faces, their children on-stage, splendid costumes, and real smiles, my deeper stream? All these men and women of corn and beans among beer-and-whitebread downtowners, mingling with rancho own-ers—my deeper stream?

Climbing to Alejandro's house up the eroded gully/trail in midnight darkness, alone, it begins to rain.

Two Barefoot Girls

Finally it occurs to me that any stream, even my "deeper stream," must have a beginning and an end; my approach in this book so far has been to present random, present-moment snapshots of events as if they were disjointed from any stream. Now, still trying to focus on a deeper stream, let me recall for you the flow of events that has brought me to Tamazunchale.

In the summer of 1971, on my first trip beyond the state of Kentucky for more than a couple of days, I was a college undergraduate hitchhiking on the Pan American Highway, on my way to spend a week at the Museum of Anthropology in Mexico City. Above the town of Tamán, ten minutes south of here, right where the highway begins its long ascent up the altiplano's slope, I met two small barefoot girls; they were carrying jugs of water to their father, who was cutting firewood up the slope.

The girls, ages eleven and nine, were Paulina and María. (María now lives two plots below Alejandro.) Curious about the gringo wearing a backpack, they asked me where I was going; with a few Spanish words and much gesturing of hands, I told them, and then proposed that I take their picture; later I'd send them a copy.

After receiving the picture Paulina, the eldest, wrote back telling how poor they were, and asking for a few pesos. I sent a small check. In a later letter Paulina explained how with that money her mother had bought a pan and begun earning pesos washing clothing for other families. Since those early years many letters have been exchanged; many checks have been sent and somehow almost every year I've managed to come for a visit, usually staying for no more than two or three hours.

When my father died in 1976, mostly to take my mother's mind off her sadness my former wife and I brought her here in a little yellow Volkswagen. Alejandro and his family still lived in Tamán, not ten feet off the Pan American Highway, in a structure about ten feet wide and twenty feet long, consisting of a rusty tin roof suspended on four poles, with a dirt floor and no walls.

I remember sitting with my mother and my wife on tiny homemade chairs while Alejandro nervously squeezed orange juice for us. During that visit Alejandro was working for a fruit wholesaler, counting oranges brought down from the mountains by Indians. My mother, who had never traveled much out of McLean County, Kentucky, and who had worked since she was a young girl as a clerk in a small-town drugstore, trying to communicate with Alejandro, the Nahuatl Indian trying to make a new life in the mestizo world . . .

In 1980 my marriage broke up, and I passed through with another woman. I remember how on the night we arrived it rained hard and while climbing the slope to Alejandro's I fell in the mud and later found myself sitting in the darkness of Alejandro's candle-lit house—this house in Tamazunchale— covered with mud, sweating heavily, and still breathing hard from my ascent, with my very inadequate Spanish trying to explain what I was doing here with another woman; I tried to make it sound as if I wasn't doing anything so wrong; several times when they asked, "But where is Rosa?" I broke down crying.

In 1982 I got a letter from Alejandro saying that his wife was dying and that they needed five hundred U.S. dollars for an operation. In short, her life was in my hands. At that time I was trying to get established as a writer; I made most of my money working part-time at the minimum wage, painting houses. A friend agreed to send $300, and I sent $200.

Later Alejandro sent a brief note saying that his wife was well, and thanks. In my next visit Alejandro's own marriage was breaking up. Climbing to the hut I found his wife. When she saw me, she handed me a banana and left, saying nothing about our saving her life. During that visit I found Alejandro's house newly hooked up with electricity; also he owned a small black-and-white TV with a broken case, a radio, and several other items I hadn't seen before, such as an electric blender. No one said anything about the operation or the money; I just let it slide.

After that visit Alejandro's wife moved back to her parents' home in Tamán and converted from Catholicism to *evangelismo.* Some of the children went with her, some stayed with him, some went back and forth, and some sometimes lived with "wives" and "husbands" who came and went.

This is the state in which Alejandro's household finds itself during my present visit. I think that Alejandro likes the idea of having a gringo as a friend, but probably my being a proven and potential source for income may color his behavior toward me. The children seem genuinely to like me.

But, still, I'm the gringo living incongruously in the

kitchen, the relatively unsocial gringo who works all the time or takes long walks, the gringo reading the Mozart book, studying Chinese, putting chlorine into water that they drink right from the buckets, the gringo who will not eat meat. . . .

I do not pretend that here I have been accepted, or even that now no tension exists around my presence. But I am paying my rent, and everyone respects that.

The Shoemaker of Avocado Alley

his slope, the road to Tetlama, and my recent walk
to Querétaro have destroyed my shoes; they simply
disintegrated. So last week I left their remains with
an old-time shoemaker at the mouth of Avocado
Alley. I asked that sandals be built on top of the soles, for the
soles still provide good arch supports for my flat feet. Today
I visit the shoemaker, whose name is Don Pancho, to pick up
my new sandals.

Having been looking into Tamazunchale's history, while
I'm sitting watching Don Pancho make some alterations, it
occurs to me that maybe this very old man can recall something interesting for me. At first his replies to my queries
seem completely inadequate and irrelevant to my questions,
but then I decide that maybe what he's saying is appropriate
after all.

"Yes, almost all my life I've lived right here in Tamazunchale," he says. His hair is white and he's developed a profoundly humped back, perhaps from having hunched over
shoes for so many years. Probably he's about eighty.

"But I've gone to the Other Side (the United States) quite a lot," he continues, smiling broadly and pushing back his straw hat so he can see me better. "I've had eighteen contracts and completed them all. Yes, I've picked a lot of cotton in Texas. But I don't speak a word of English. Just Spanish. Of course I do understand Nahuatl, but I can't speak it very well. Not long ago, in the river down by Tamán, a group of gringos came speaking English, looking for the treasure there. They say that part of Montezuma's treasure lies there in an iron box this big—*gold*, you know. Those gringos, they diverted the river with big machines, then left all of a sudden. People say that the gringos got the gold and went in the middle of the night so that the Mexican people wouldn't get any of it. My God, man, what huge feet you have. I've never had to make shoes like these."

Now his smile grows broader, he puts down my sandals

and walks around his table, which lies cluttered with old shoes, scraps of leather, and bottles of nails, dyes, and polish.

"I'll bet the women like you," he suggests inquiringly. "We know that the gringos have real long peckers and that they make their women real happy. We Mexicans, we just have little things that hardly get the job done."

His three young apprentices who so far have kept in the background working silently and diligently now break into huge laughter.

"That was my problem," he continues. "Those women. I'd come back from the Other Side with my pockets full of money, but then I'd spend everything I had in Monterrey, having fun with women. When I'd get back to Tamazunchale, I'd be as poor as when I left. Ah, if I'd been equipped like a gringo, those women would have paid *me* and I'd be a rich man now. Ay, I've never seen feet like yours, man."

Incident at the Super Tortilladora

t the Super Tortilladora I'm standing in line behind six Indian-type women when this relatively
fair-skinned, fifty-year-old mestiza (mixed Indian
and European) waltzes in, goes to the front of the
line, and tells the Indian girl weighing the tortillas to give her
half a kilo. The Indian girl does it, ignoring those of us waiting our turn.

From the Super Tortilladora I head for the one place in
town from which I can make a long-distance telephone call—
a little booth in the corner of a restaurant. One Indian girl
about twelve years old is handling all calls. She's sitting there
with a large patch on her blouse, wearing a skirt made of a
black sack stitched together by someone working very fast.
She's trying her best to raise the long-distance operator in
another town, but usually there's simply no answer, so she
just sits there dialing 02 again and again. I stand for an hour
before I realize that the few calls getting through are being
made for people who came in *after* I did but who demanded
that their calls be made *right then*. My call isn't completed
until the very last, apparently because I terrorize the girl less
vigorously than the others.

These are not isolated incidents. When I'm buying first-class bus tickets in large terminals throughout Mexico, it's not unusual for people to cut in front of me. At the markets as I'm talking with merchants about prices, people simply interpose themselves between the merchant and me and do their business while I wait for another turn.

Those who cut in ahead of me are seldom Indians; almost always they are people who consider themselves to be middle-class, or even aspire to being upper class. Of course, the real upper class never cut in. Maybe it's because they do not frequent places with lines; I don't know.

This cutting-in is pretty standard throughout most of Latin America. During my first trip to Mexico City in 1971, I needed to take a bus from the city center to the outskirts. However, when *every* bus came along, people crowded in front of me until all the bus's standing space was taken, and then the door slammed in my face. This happened five times; then I walked over twenty miles, working off my rage, swearing that I'd never return to Mexico again.

I used to think that the cutting in might be an expression of anti-U. S. sentiment, which often is very strong in Latin America. But then I noticed that even soft-spoken, unpushy Mexicans, especially the Indians, suffered the same indignities as I. Nonetheless, my being a gringo does enter into the equation.

The cutting-in-front phenomenon became even more inexplicable when I discovered that most, if not almost all, pushers are just regular people who under normal circumstances are very pleasant. Several times I've become acquainted with individual Latins whom I recognized as earlier having aggressively cut in front of me. The moment we established eye contact and exchanged pleasantries, they became gracious and accommodating.

156

In general, where Indians and mestizos exist side by side, race enters the picture. The lighter your skin, the greater your license to expect your need for convenience to prevail over that of others. Often the white-skinned people don't even have to shove, for Indians generally yield without resistance. Recently in Guatemala I saw an old Indian woman on a second-class bus automatically relinquish her seat when a much younger, fair-skinned mestiza woman entered the bus and stood beside her. The young mestiza did not even thank the old Indian. Such perversions of etiquette certainly are not the norm here, but they are common enough to be a conspicuous feature of the culture.

Another of the subtleties of the cut-in phenomenon expressed itself a few years back when I was trying to buy a train ticket in Monterrey. Four people in a row had cut in front of me when I was talking with the ticket agent. They simply shoved in front of me as words were coming from my mouth, demanded a ticket, and got it. The fifth cutter-in I gently picked up and set to one side. He became so outraged that I feared his having a heart attack; others standing around us hardly acted less resentful.

Thus, my strategy now is this: Just let them walk all over me; treat it as a kind of yoga designed to instill self-discipline and humility.

But, I repeat, very seldom do you see the Indians cutting in.

A Community Project

More than once in this book I've used judgmental gringo phrases to describe conditions in Colonia el Sacrificio. For a while I've been thinking that maybe I need to temper these judgments; let me tell you about the gravel pile.

For several weeks a truckload of black, sandy gravel has been dumped as far up Avocado Alley as a truck could back, right in the path's middle. During all that time each member of Colonia el Sacrificio's society has had to climb over the pile each time a visit was made downtown.

Roosters perched on it and pigs rooted in it; kids played in it, scattering it. Its sudden appearance where it seemed to have no right to be, and its subsequent gradual deterioration, was so in character with all other phenomena in the valley that it never even occurred to me to wonder what it was doing there, or to consider it a shame that the pile was being spread out and mingled with the slope's general debris.

Then one Saturday afternoon a three-by-four-foot chalkboard was hung on a large royal poinciana tree growing in the path's middle. On the board stood a message from "The

Committee" reading, "Tomorrow, Sunday, from 8:30 A.M. to 2:00 P.M., gravel will be carried from the pile below to here. The objective will be to build cement steps."

The cement steps already in place have always fascinated me. They begin more or less at the gravel pile and climb steeply for about 300 feet, broken here and there where the ground levels out. It's easy to see that over the years they've been created by various squads of workers. Each "project" is about ten feet long. Some series of steps are well made, with uniform steps and solid concrete, but others are already falling apart. In some places the steps are of such irregular spacing that it's confusing to walk up them—you have to concentrate to keep from tripping.

I arrive at the sign on the royal poinciana tree at nine o'clock Sunday morning, assuming that even though I'm half an hour late I'll be the first there; but, to my vast surprise,

159

half a dozen men have already been at work for half an hour. Their surprise in seeing el gringo show up and offer help is also vast.

"But you need a can, a burlap bag, and a mecapál," they say. A mecapál is a loop of rope equipped with a flat burlap strap that fits atop your head. The idea is to string the rope around the can, place the burlap bag as a cushion between your back and the can filled with gravel, and with the burlap ribbon across your head, carry the burden on your back. Alejandro has a Sunday-morning date with his young girlfriend, Martha, so I return to the house, and Lolín helps me get the items together. Then for three hours I carry load after load of gravel up the slope. Each rectangular can of moist, sandy gravel weighs about eighty pounds.

It is true that my idea of "work" and theirs is different. Usually they carry one or two loads, then rest and talk for up to half an hour, or else take on another task such as chopping down the lovely royal poinciana that they say is in the way but which easily could be bypassed. As I see it, the main job is hauling gravel, so I begin doing that with ten-minute breaks every hour. I think that with this routine I'm generous to myself, but it seems to disconcert my fellow workers.

"Take a break, man," they keep saying. But when I do sit down to rest, I'm not really interested in sharing their conversation; I am a man with a mission. And, anyway, I welcome the exercise. I work up a good sweat, the black sand soon sticks prodigiously to my legs, arms and back, and quickly I become a spectacle for all passersby.

I quit at noon, feeling that I've done at least my share; the others stay and work on and off for the rest of the day, sipping whiskey, from time to time working frenetically, and then taking extended rests. The thing is, the job does get finished. The steps turn out to be neither the best "project" nor the worst. When later I pass by the finished product, I have to stand for a moment and reflect:

I came and put in my hours and did a great deal of work. I went home fagged out; they went home tipsy and laughing, also convinced that they too had put in a hard day of work and wondering why in the world el gringo had practically killed himself. Just to show off, they probably thought.

But, I wouldn't have felt right doing it any way but my way. And I suspect that neither would they.

The Austrian

ately I've been thinking about my Austrian friend, Dieter. He's spent much of his life bouncing between Vienna and various Latin American destinations. We first met on a balcony in Guatemala City about fifteen years ago. Just in from Austria, he had much to say about the uptight society from which he'd recently escaped:

"We German speakers drive everything into the ground," he complained. "We like to be neat, so we make a million neatness laws and everyone goes around puckered up and afraid he'll do something not neat. We've forgotten how to be spontaneous, how to be natural. We're machines programmed for efficiency. You get on a tram in Vienna and it's just a bunch of old people with gray faces staring into empty space. But, here . . ."

He waved his arm in an arc that took in everything from the traffic-jammed street below the balcony to the volcano on the horizon spewing out black ash.

"Here people can be themselves," he continued. "If someone really wants to fart, he farts! I should like to fart sometimes, but my German blood and upbringing forbid it. Who says I shouldn't fart? If I could, I'd fart right now, just to announce to my body that here it's okay. Just look down below at how *alive* those people are."

Three months later we were back on the same balcony. Now Dieter had changed his tune:

"When I get back to Vienna the first thing I'll do," he swore, "is to find a bench next to a traffic light, and I'll just sit watching all the cars stop when the light turns red. I'm so sick of all this childish, self-indulgent, every-person-doing-his-own-thing Latin behavior. And though I still believe that much of the poverty here results from past and present U.S. or European imperialism, now I just have to wonder why I never meet Latins capable of calmly thinking things out. Sometimes I'm convinced that nobody in this country has a serious, well-developed thought in his head."

Of course, not long afterward I got a letter from Dieter in Vienna saying how hard he was working to get back to Latin America where he could unbutton his collar again and think natural thoughts.

I'm thinking of Dieter these days because often I tend to be like him. In the States I wanted to "immerse myself" in Mexico. Yet this morning I've spent a considerable amount of energy fuming over people spitting where I have to walk. *Hack! Patooey!* The people here don't care where they spit.

Ach! What a pleasure it would be to see people stopping at a stoplight. Or just to *see* a stoplight.

A History of Tamazunchale

Somewhere, in those centuries of the ancients, probably coming from Asia across the Bering Strait, a people walked into this land calling themselves by names that now we do not know. By about 700 B.C., along Mexico's Gulf slope, certain of them had developed a culture now referred to in the books as the Olmec Civilization; the Olmecs lasted until around A.D. 300; a good guess is that they evolved into the cultures that now we refer to by such names as Aztec, Maya, and Huastec. The Huastec civilization developed in this area, in the antipleno's foothills along the Rio Moctezuma, and extended as far east as the Gulf Coast; it included land on which today we find the large port city of Tampico.

Around A.D. 1100, this Huastec land was ruled by a queen called Tomiyauh. Tradition has it that later Huastec generations began calling the town from which she had ruled Tamuxumtzalle. In Huastec, *tam* means place, *uxum* means woman, and *tzalle* means ruler. Eventually the name Tamuxumtzalle was corrupted into Tamazunchale.

In 1454, the Aztec emperor Montezuma I invaded the

Huastec region, beating the Huastecs into submission. Thereafter the Huastecs had to pay tribute to the Aztecs, whose capital was the splendid city called Tenochitlán, high on the altiplano about 150 air miles south of here, on a well-fortified island in the large lake called Lake Texcoco. Now this site is the dusty land occupied by Mexico City.

Several times the Huastecs unsuccessfully rebelled against the Aztecs; several times the Aztecs sent war parties into this region collecting victims to serve as human sacrifices during the Aztecs' religious ceremonies.

In 1521 Tenochitlán, now ruled by Montezuma II, fell to the Spanish conquistador Hernán Cortés. In 1522 Cortés, with 120 cavalry, 300 foot soldiers, and 40,000 Indian fighters, passed down the long-established trail from Tenochitlán to the Gulf port city of Pánuco, passing through Tamazunchale. They had to fight 60,000 Huastecs to get through, but they managed.

The next year Spanish soldiers committed such atrocities in the Huastec region that the Huastecs rebelled, killing 300 Spaniards. In 1524, Cortés sent fifty cavalry, 100 Spanish foot soldiers, and 30,000 Indian fighters to punish the Huastecs. Part of the punishment meted out was the burning of 400 of the Huastecs' principal leaders. The entire Huastec population in and around Tamazunchale and Tamán was extirpated; today if you wish to hear Huastec spoken you must visit Ciudad Valles, about fifty miles to the north of Tamazunchale.

I can't find a definitive statement about why Nahuatl speakers instead of someone else occupied this land once the Huastecs were gone. The Nahuatl language is very closely related to Aztec, and more than one expert considers them to be mere dialects of the same language. Therefore I speculate that during the years when the Aztecs were forcing the

Huastecs to pay tribute, the Aztecs maintained outposts here. Later, when the Aztec capital itself fell under the onslaught of Cortés, many Aztecs must have fled here, seeking to begin new lives.

In 1550, in accordance with the *encomienda* system with which the Spanish distributed land and Indians to their countrymen, Tamazunchale was granted to a man called Juan de Cervantes; at that time the town consisted of 102 mostly Nahuatl-speaking families.

Then for many decades things drifted along, the Indians contributing what amounted to slave labor and the Spanish doing what they pleased.

A legal document from 1746 shows that at that time Tamazunchale consisted of thirty-six Spanish families and 358 Indian families.

In 1811, hearing that Mexican independence from Spain had been declared by Hidalgo, Tamazunchalens promptly rebelled against the town's Spanish occupiers. In 1812, after several skirmishes between royalists (pro-Spanish) and independence-minded Mexicans, the town was burned. Rebuilding took years, but afterward Tamazunchale stayed in Mexican hands. Mexican independence finally was achieved in 1823.

In 1861, Tamazunchale sent a number of fighters to help defend Mexico against the United States, which was invading from the north. The gringos had Manifest Destiny on their minds; they wanted more land for themselves. After losing this war, the Mexicans were obliged to renounce all claim to land that today makes up the states of Texas, California, New Mexico, Arizona, Nevada, Utah, and part of Colorado.

In 1862, rival political parties fighting for control of Tamazunchale succeeded in burning the town for a second time.

In 1879, eight hundred Indians banned together and with shotguns, bows and arrows, spears, slingshots, and bayonets fixed on sticks attacked a government barracks in Tamazunchale, killing two soldiers, wounding others, and scattering the rest. Looting followed and demands were made of certain big landowners. Some landowners were spread on top of anthills; one old man died among the ants. This Indian uprising lasted from 1879 to 1881.

In 1914, with yet another set of rival political parties fighting for control of Tamazunchale, the town was burned for the third time.

A big flood hit here in 1955.

I'd passed the building several times but until today I'd never noticed that on the wall someone had painted the words BIBLIOTECA PÚBLICA MUNICIPAL MANUEL JOSE OTHON; these words announce the presence of a library. Entering the modest-looking building I anticipated finding a few hundred out-of-date volumes in crates, lorded over by a town eccentric.

However, inside I beheld many thousands of mostly new, very fine books; the above information about Tamazunchale's history was gleaned from them. With reverence this morning I read the *Monografía de Tamazunchale* by Professor Sixto García Pacheco and a photocopied 1894 classic by Macedonia Acosta called *Ligeros Apuntes para la Historia Política de Tamazunchale.* Also on the shelves were recently published encyclopedias, dictionaries for various languages, many volumes on Mexico's indigenous populations, books of poetry, fine novels, books on geography, music, opera, art history, market analysis, horticulture. . . . Around me were the complete works of Jorge Luis Borges, Homer's *Iliad* . . .

Just as the filth and anarchy were about to win, along came this library with its serious visitors, its well-lighted reading area, and its librarian who really seemed to know where all the books were. The librarian was a small young woman of Indian descent. I complimented her on the library.

"The federal government is establishing a network of fine libraries all through the Republic," she replied softly, proudly, and in perfect, respectable Spanish.

Lolín's Three Dreams

Now that Paulina, her husband, and three girls have moved out, and all the men more or less work at outside jobs, Lolín is the person I'm around most. Seldom leaving the house, she has prime responsibilities for preparing all meals and for washing all the men's clothes. (I feed myself and wash my own clothes, though I do pay Lolín 2000 pesos a week for supplying me with one cup of black beans each day.)

Lolín tells me that she's very unhappy, and that her long, uneventful days here fill her with despair. Sergio lives with Lolín; at least when things are going well between them, they consider themselves to be married. Often Sergio is away at night, ostensibly working at odd jobs in other towns.

Before Sergio came along, for several months Lolín lived with a man in Tamán. However, when she didn't become pregnant, the man left her, saying he wanted a woman who could produce children. Lolín has been trying to get pregnant with Sergio but without success; she's afraid that Sergio also might leave. Therefore, more than anything, Lolín yearns to have a baby. She's asked the healer from Matlapa about herbs to cure her apparent barrenness, but for that cure the healer demands a price too high to pay.

Lolín has heard me say that I enjoy interpreting other people's dreams, so recently she began bringing her most vivid dreams to me. Here are the three I've heard so far:

Dream #1: "I was at my wedding, feeling very happy. But when I looked at my groom, he wasn't Sergio or anyone else I knew. Then the ceremony began and it turned out that the man already was married, so we had to forget the whole thing."

Dream #2: "I was standing in the doorway of this house not doing anything special. Then I saw an old man coming. It was Sergio's father. In his arms he was carrying snow. Sergio's father is dead, and seeing him coming toward me with white snow scared me a lot."

Dream #3: "My father climbed up that *ciruela* tree behind the big kitchen, trying to pick some fruits. But the tree fell down and Papa died. I cried and cried."

I interpret each of these dreams as being expressions of Lolín's desire to bear children, and of her fear that she is barren.

In the first dream her maternal instincts are frustrated by the most ego-shattering revelation possible for a woman looking forward to marriage and family—not only that her lover cannot marry her but that during the entire courtship he has been married to another woman. In the second dream, the snow in Sergio's dead father's arms symbolizes Lolín's barrenness. Significantly, the old man approaches as Lolín stands in the doorway—at the threshold. It is the pregnancy threshold across which she must pass before she can find fulfillment but which her being barren may prevent.

When Lolín told me about the third dream, the *ciruela* tree was absolutely full of persimmon-size, orange-yellow fruits falling day and night onto my tin roof. In the dream the *ciruela* tree represents nothing less than the Tree of Life. Alejandro's climbing into it symbolizes Lolín's yearnings to see her family, through her, perpetuated. But the tree collapses, her father (representing her family's perpetuation) dies, and all is lost.

Lolín's family-oriented dreams take on a special poignancy when viewed in the context of this slope's sociological realities. Here women's responsibilities are precisely defined, and there's not much room for nonstandard female roles. Women have babies, take care of children, prepare food, and wash clothes. Mature women not participating in these specific duties usually endure a very low status.

Alien Thoughts

Walking along the Rio Moctezuma, I pause to sit on a rock. No rain has fallen for eight days so now the heat is not as oppressively humid as it has been. The morning air smells good and somehow makes me feel more alive than usual. Beyond these mountains the sky shows the kind of dark blue that in Kentucky we associate with October's cool, dry days; clustered next to the highest peaks are white cumulus clouds with lead-gray bottoms.

On the mountain slopes above, cornfields are showing up in places where all summer I thought secondary forests still were surviving. In the summer the corn's green color was the same as the greenness of surrounding woods, but now the corn is maturing and turning straw-colored; now the mountains are patched, just like the clothes of the Indians who plant the corn.

This river runs through a valley with massive, distinctly layered, highly fractured, gray limestone cliffs. A hawk circles in the sky. It's one of those gauzy, harp-and-violins moments; I feel *soul stroked* by the land around me.

Why should all this please me so greatly? Not only, "Why am *I* put together in such a way that this pleases me?" but, also, "Why is *all this* put together in such a way that it pleases me?"

I suspect that in other worlds other forms of intelligence exist. I'll bet that if those beings somehow could be transported to beside me right now, they might find themselves being intellectually stimulated by what we can behold around us, and they might react positively or negatively to certain stimuli, but never, I believe, would they feel soul stroked.

Having evolved under environmental conditions different from that of us humans, if my extraterrestrial visitor had eyes, those eyes probably would not be sensitive to the same region of the electromagnetic spectrum as mine. Instead of seeing white clouds floating harmoniously in a blue sky,

173

maybe they'd see a blinding glare of infrared radiation with no clouds at all; maybe they'd see the wind's vortices and streams where I see nothing but emptiness. Maybe they'd be unable to see water in the Rio Moctezuma. Whatever they beheld, I doubt that they would feel in harmony with what they saw—not the way I do, right now.

But, see, *my* species has evolved here—here on this earth. These green slopes, this blue sky, streaming water, and these ancient layers of earth are precisely the things from which I come.

The Space Shuttle

Today on the road to Tetlama I carry in my knapsack the small shortwave radio that accompanies me during all my foreign travels. Climbing up through weedy fields of corn and nopal, I watch the time; a little before the appointed moment I tune to a "Voice of America" frequency in the 19 Meter Band (a range of frequencies), around 15.30 mhz. Now I sit on a roadside rock beneath an over-arching canopy of bird-of-paradise blossoms and, gazing across the hazy Gulf lowlands toward the east, listen to Mission Control as the space shuttle *Discovery* lifts off from Cape Canaveral.

During earlier lift-offs sometimes I've been back home in Kentucky where I could watch the action on color TV; often, however, I wouldn't even bother. In the context of the suburban life-style I experience in the United States, where frequently I feel buried in plastic and isolated from people by materialism's incessant demands, a spaceship seems to be just so much more electronics and politics.

So why now as the *Discovery* lifts into the blue skies above Florida am I so thrilled? Right now why am I reminding myself of that young Indian woman in the library, sweetly filled with pride? And, most important, why this when I'm in Mexico, and not when I'm in the States?

I don't believe that it's racial pride or nationalism. I've been in Latin America so often that a lot of my own interior core feels short, black-haired, and brown-skinned; sometimes my tall, blue-eyed, and güero reflection in store windows actually surprises me. So often I've been embarrassed by the U.S. policies in Latin America that I could never be a flag waver here.

Neither is my new-found exultation because I am glad to be part of a society that is forging ahead, in contrast to what I find here. For I see plainly that this society is also rapidly evolving. The growing numbers of homes with electricity, the new radio station XEGI, new roads such as the one to Tetlama, a gradually rising literacy rate . . .

Nor is it that I am proud to be of a society of workers and achievers, whereas people here are of another kind. It is true that here typically you see many able-bodied men idle, not working. But it's also true that on an average day at least one or two men will ask me how they can acquire jobs in the States. In the park downtown if you see a small group of men animatedly talking, there's a very good chance that the topic will be jobs "On the Other Side."

In Alejandro's household, during the time I've been here, I've seen him working fairly regularly on the municipal job of constructing concrete steps. Twenty-year-old José Juan, a son who lives at home, makes about a dollar a day winding copper wire around laminated iron cores of burned-out electric-motor armatures; Lolín's Sergio makes a little money hanging around a tire-repair shop, and, when he can, he's the driver's helper in a truck that delivers oranges and bananas to other parts of the country. Twenty-two-year-old Juan, another live-at-home son, is in perfect health and aching for a job and jumps at every opportunity that comes along but ends up drifting between various relatives' houses, spending a lot of time reading semisexy adventure comics. Eighteen-year-old Gregorio, another son, has gone to Mexico City and works as a laborer for about two dollars a day.

In short, Colonia el Sacrificio's lying-around men more reflect the lack of good jobs than any innate laziness. Geopolitics and a quirky history brings on the area's inescapable mud and dung.

Nonetheless, my coming here has been for me a kind of stepping back in time. Decades ago we in the world of telephones and running water had already passed through the stage of social evolution now apparent here. Having to watch for manure on footpaths is like having to worry about acne again; for a fourteen-year old the acne experience might be character building; but as a forty-two-year-old man I do not care to deal with it.

Thus the *Discovery* space shot reminds me that in a few days I'll be back home, able to stop expending so much energy focusing on path scats, finding uncontaminated water, getting enough daily protein in my diet, fighting mildew and the odor of sour sweat, avoiding mosquitoes and black flies.

Ah, and now I happen to remember the problem: For once you're free of those distractions and enjoy so much extra time, if you're in no position to set off rockets, just exactly how do you spend that time?

A Walt Whitman Kind of Day

oint your eyes in any direction, focus, immediately close them, and then, as you digest what's in the image behind your lids, *every time* you find a busy, interesting scene to please you. Here are some examples:

Right now I'm on the municipal market's second floor, behind the waist-high cinder-block wall. I cast my eyes in a random direction and close them. I catch an obviously Nahuatl-speaking man carrying under an arm a red, woven-plastic bag with an old hen in it. The hen is red herself and, like most hens here, of the breed with a featherless neck. She's riding with her head sticking from the bag; she seems to be looking around, enjoying the scenery as it floats by. The man wears a huge smile, a smile in which the top front teeth are missing. He's barefooted and reaching out to shake someone's hand.

My second image shows an Indian woman in a pale blue dress sitting with her back against the gray cinder-block wall below me. Two braids of black hair hang upon her rounded shoulders as she hunches over, cutting slivers of nopal cactus onto a flat section of glossy banana leaf lying on her lap. Later the nopal shavings will be sold in small plastic bags to people who will fry them for the dish called *nopalitos.*

The third image is of a young man wearing sandals and a green T-shirt that proclaims OHIO STATE; he directs a red pickup filled with yellow-green bananas as it backs up. An old dog lying in the street gets up to escape the oncoming truck; the dog looks over its shoulder in apparent annoyance.

A fourth image comes exactly in front of me, from the second floor of the building across the street. On her balcony a mestiza woman waters twenty or so potted plants. She wears a frowsy red slip that looks like something she's been sleeping in. The wall behind her is October-sky blue while the wall below is Irish green.

Now I let my eyes wander, cataloging the town:

At an open-air butcher shop, plucked yellow chickens dangle by thin-stretched necks. Then along the street, green achote squash spread on a black towel, yellow-orange corn kernels heaped a foot high on a brown sheet of paper, dark brown slabs of copal resin wrapped in straw-colored corn husks (incense used since pre-Columbian times), in a silvery cage hung on a green wall, green parrots with red and yellow head markings.

An old man peeling a green orange, a boy leaning against a palm tree's whitewashed trunk, a little girl with a book wrapped in brown paper, a black dog sulking beneath a red pickup, gray-and-white pigeons soaring overhead, an Indian with a load of firewood on his back and a bouquet of gladioluses, a boy throwing a rope over another rope strung across the street, about to pull up a blue plastic sheet to protect from rain the hardware he'll display below on top of a sheet of plywood resting on homemade wooden sawhorses, an old woman with two long gray braids and a pink dress leaving the Super Tortilladora with a kilo of tortillas wrapped in pinkish brown paper.

Not a single gray tone here, no person soft and mediocre looking, no one bored, and the ones who look crazy obviously are not that way because of existential conflicts! I walk down the streets drinking all this in, suddenly hungry for more and more, suddenly covetous of all about me.

Look at the color! Look at this riotous circus and hear its laughter!

And what if I had a lover here, down at the end of this street? Camomile tea brewing and words of understanding and touches of papaya sweetness and smiles of upside-down yellow bananas on curved stalks beneath arching, glossy leaves . . . ?

Demographics

O f all the books in Tamazunchale's library, probably none speaks more succinctly on the whys and whens of Mexico than *México Demográfico*, published in 1981 by the *Consejo Nacional de Población*. Today I sit thumbing through it, its numbers and graphs correlating in my mind with images and incidents from these last weeks. Here are some randomly chosen bits of information:

Between 1900 and 1950, Mexico's population doubled to about 25.8 million. During the twenty years between 1950 and 1970, it doubled again, to 50.7 million.

In 1940, the life expectancy of a Mexican male was 40.4 years; for a Mexican woman, 42.5. In 1970, the expectancy had risen to 60.0 and 64.0 years for males and females, respectively.

In 1980, considering adults fifteen and above, seventy-nine percent of all Mexicans were regarded as being able to read.

In 1980, in San Luis Potosí, about 287,500 family occupied units were counted, of which about seventy-nine percent were owned by the people living in them. About forty-nine percent had electricity, about fifty-one percent had running

water, about twenty-nine percent had their sewage disposal
system hooked into a larger municipal system, about fifty-six
percent of the dwellings were two or more stories high, about
thirty percent were of brick or block, about thirty-six percent
were of adobe, and about twenty-seven percent were of
wood, bamboo, or such. (The high adobe rate reflects the fact
that most of San Luis Potosí is high-elevation, arid desert,
unlike the moist lowland environment in which Tamazunchale is located.)

One of the most interesting charts compares Mexico's
demographics with those of other nations. Here I've reduced
the chart to show only the comparisons between Mexico,
the United States, and Switzerland:

	POPULATION	GROWTH RATE	PERCENT URBAN	MALE LIFE EXPECTANCY
Mexico	65,432,000	3.2	64.4	62.3 (1980)
United States	218,059,000	0.7	73.5	68.7 (1975)
Switzerland	6,330,000	-0.4	54.6	70.3 (1970)

Moreover, on page 183 is a graph I've fixed up using numbers from this book; the points on this graph cause in my
mind powerful echoes of Colonia el Sacrificio's hordes of children coughing and crying in the night, laughing from behind
bushes, clapping with XEGI's music in the afternoon . . . children, children, everywhere.

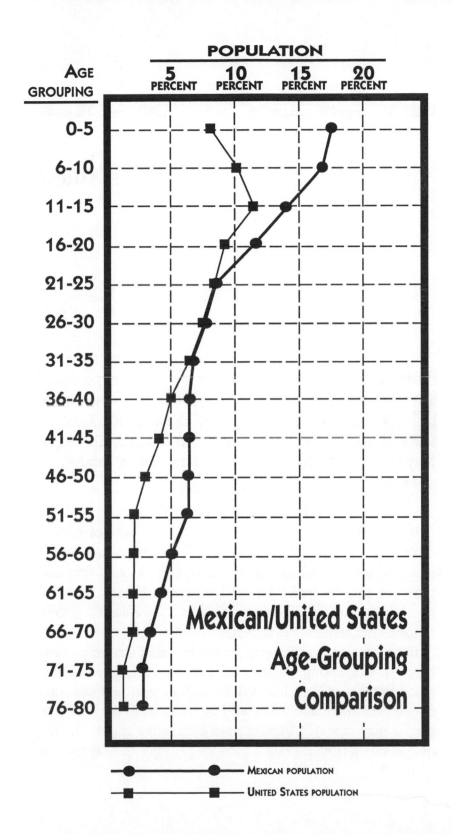

POPULATION

| AGE GROUPING | 5 PERCENT | 10 PERCENT | 15 PERCENT | 20 PERCENT |

Mexican/United States Age-Grouping Comparison

●————● MEXICAN POPULATION
■————■ UNITED STATES POPULATION

Six Portraits

This book is ending. Walking through Tamazun-chale's streets, I find myself regretting certain omissions from the story that's been told. Curiously, all the omissions seem to deal with people. Maybe I just needed until now to draw certain conclusions about them.

Bernardo Hernández

Back in Agua Zarca, Bernardo was the husband of Alejandro's sister, Gregoria; he accompanied Alejandro and me the morning we walked to the Rio Tancuilín. Around fifty-five years of age, he looks like a completely average Nahuatl speaker. But during the twenty-four hours we were together, twice he did remarkable things.

In the afternoon of the day Alejandro and I arrived in Agua Zarca, I was taking pictures of Bernardo's family as they stood in front of their hut. While fiddling with my camera, I noticed that Bernardo was standing away from the others in such a way that they couldn't see him, but I could. Though he had taken from his belt a foot-long dagger, the dagger was not what caught my attention. It was Bernardo's face. Forcing a stagy smile, he arched his eyebrows unnaturally high and, with his face directed downward toward his dagger, had his eyes screwed around, riveted on me. It was like a dramatic instant in a highly stylized Japanese Noh play. When he saw me looking, his eyes swung down to his dagger, for a split second he looked at his dagger in precisely the same manner a mother looks at her newborn child, and then swiftly and furtively he sheathed the blade behind his belt. Then he returned to stand with his family.

Apparently my own glance had been so fleeting that he thought I'd missed seeing him. For in about a minute, the entire pantomime was reenacted, exactly as before. However, this time I let him catch me looking; then he returned to his place in line, where he stood erect instead of slouching as usual, and now he wore a handsomely self-assured expression. He seemed an altogether different person.

Really I don't know what was on Bernardo's mind during these displays. Probably he just wanted to show a gringo that even he deserved a little respect. However, I had shown no lack of respect previously.

The second poignant moment occurred when we arrived on the Tancuilín's banks. Bernardo walked upstream about fifty yards, completely disrobed, and waded across the shallows to water deep enough to swim in. As he waded he created a silhouette against the shimmering, rippling shoal behind him. His legs were short and knotty; his chest, for his height, was massive. Being right then in real jungle next to a pristine wild river, his image passing before me seemed impossibly primitive and ancient. When later he returned wearing his patched and sweat-stained peasant's clothes, I just had to walk near him to ask a few pointless questions about the river and forest; I wished to savor speaking with this man

185

who only moments earlier had seemed millions of years away.

My Host in Tetitla

I left out part of the story about my host in Tetitla. After I had been invited to stay overnight, but before we actually reached his house, my host proposed we stop for a beer in a thatch-roofed hut selling drinks at very high prices—expensive because everything had to be carried in on mules or people's backs. I thanked my host but declined; finally I came to understand that he wanted me to buy *him* a beer. I felt obligated to do so—even though a single small beer cost the equivalent of what for him was half a day's wages.

I intended to sit with him, but before I could enter the hut a tiny chair was brought out to the hut's muddy courtyard where I was invited to rest and wait in the company of some rooting pigs. After my host had been inside for a few minutes, he returned to me and with a funny look on his face said, "It's double the price."

I interpreted the situation as being that the price of beer had doubled without his knowing it and that he was embarrassed to find himself without enough money. I forked over another handful of pesos. When he went back inside, I heard a second bottle being opened. As we left the bar, I felt resentful that I'd been tricked, but I said nothing. After all, for me the money was not that important, and everyone needs to splurge once in a while.

Later that night, in front of his wife, his *carnal,* and his compadre, my host said this: "My little boy is very ill; will you give me money for his medicine?" The child looked well to me and I felt strongly that I'd been put on the spot intentionally, so that I'd be too embarrassed to refuse paying for the child's medicine.

186

However, for me, this second deceit was too much. I revealed that I knew about the second beer trick, which he didn't deny, and I said that I understood how he was trying to manipulate me before his family and friends; neither did he deny this. The man looked as if he'd been struck by lightning. I got up to leave; his wife, though unable to speak in Spanish, understood enough to comprehend what had happened, and she gave a grunt that even I recognized as meaning that under no circumstances should I, their guest, be allowed to leave under such a dark cloud.

So I sat back down, we talked things out, and I agreed to stay if my host would agree to stop manipulating me into money-giving situations. For the rest of my stay both of us acted as if nothing negative had happened.

I am biased in favor of people who live close to the land, but I tell you about this incident in an effort to be honest about what I'm seeing here: Indians, in the end, are just like the rest of us.

Paulina

Paulina, the eldest of Alejandro's daughters, is one of the original "two barefoot girls" I met in 1971, and the mother of Martha, Nanaya, and Marcela.

A few months after Martha, her first baby, was born, I passed through. Alejandro and his wife had taken over Martha's rearing. This state of affairs endured for so many years that to this day Martha calls Alejandro Papá and his wife Mamá.

One afternoon during a more recent visit, I was sitting with the family as Paulina spooned hot broth to one of her babies. She was blowing in order to cool off the soup. But, the thing is, her stream of air was passing far above the soup's surface. Paulina thought that the act of blowing, with

the spoon held in the general vicinity—in and of itself—
cooled off hot soup.

During my present visit Paulina has risen in my estima-
tion. Now at least she's doing a better job when it comes to
taking care of her three children. She also works very hard
washing other people's clothes for a fee; often at night her
back muscles ache so severely and her hands are so chapped
that she cannot sleep.

Pancho, her husband, moved the family from Alejandro's
place into a small, pole-walled hut next to the river. Promptly
the river flooded and they lost many of their possessions.
Paulina's friends and family tell her to leave Pancho. She
makes excuses about why she must stay a little longer, and
when she runs out of excuses she simply admits that she
loves the man. I have always admired people who love, even
when it appears to be dumb love.

Visiting Paulina now is a sad experience. From head to toe the whole family is covered with silver-dollar-sized sores; the doctor says it's a fungal infection caught from the river's mud. The medicine I bought for them is white and pasty, so when the family walks down the street they look like a troupe of harlequins. During the flood the water rose to about four feet deep in their hut; now they and their hut smell fishy. The river is still muddy, so when Paulina washes clothes in it, no matter how much soap and bleach she uses, the clothes come out dingy-looking.

Sometimes I think that Paulina considers me to be a kind of powerful, beautiful big brother. Having never had a brother or sister, and seldom in my life having been the object of adulation, she gives me a funny feeling.

Lolín

Of all the people here, twenty-one-year-old Lolín is the one I've been around most. During my first month beneath the cocuite tree, she often came to sit beside my tent to talk. "Tell me something," she'd say, and then for a few minutes I'd talk about snowy winters in Kentucky or riding trains in Europe. During this last month, each day at noon when I returned from my walks, she'd usually be at the house alone. As I typed in the afternoon, she'd frequently interrupt me for chats; several evenings we've been at the house by ourselves. She sits with me beneath the porch's single lightbulb while I study Chinese.

Lolín is the most "natural" person I've ever known. If she's upset, she bawls like a young calf with a stomachache. If a stranger wanders along the path below the toilet, either she'll rush out to the embankment to watch, as if she were a suspicious watchdog, or else she'll simply yell, "Hey! What do you want up here?" With her sisters she gossips interminably and she lies whenever it's convenient. Her lies are so disingenuous that you see right through them. When she's caught in an awkward social situation she animatedly scratches her ribs, rolling her stomach around as if it were a pile of jelly. She curses obscenely, spits with little precision, and when—after reading her trashy novelettes—she gets horny, you can feel the steam.

Alejandro

Once my daily routine in Tamazunchale crystallized, most days passed without my even seeing Alejandro. Usually I was on the road to Tetlama before any of the family was out of bed; at night I'd be inside my mosquito net listening to the shortwave before Alejandro came in from work, a little after 8:00 P.M. Mostly I saw Alejandro only on rainy days when he couldn't work, and sometimes on Sunday mornings before he went off with Martha.

Alejandro seems to have a flare for small-time politics. He loves to say things like, "If I need a passport, all I have to do is to talk with my friend, Juan Fulano." He reminds me of the county highway department employees back in Kentucky who land patronage jobs sitting in pickup trucks watching others mow grass and pick up trash—except that Alejandro does appear to work.

During our years together I've seen Alejandro evolve from being a timid, ragged Indian from the mountains into a fairly respected member of mestizo-land—one with a considerably younger girlfriend, who has cut quite a few capers with him in the streets below. During this trip my impression of Alejandro has been enlarged.

I don't like the way Alejandro walks into the kitchen after being away all day and simply says, "Lolín, get me some food," without so much as a "please," a smile, or a pat on the back. However, it seems that most men here in the Colonia

190

treat their wives and daughters the same way. Similarly, I despise his spitting habits, but also that's a typical habit of people here, even of many women. Besides, maybe these habits are no worse than our tendency in the States to pay women less than men for work of equal value; and U.S. cigarette smokers who smoke around nonsmokers aren't any more sophisticated than Mexican spitters.

Despite these matters, I still like Alejandro. It's been a long road from being a Nahuatl-speaking kid in Agua Zarca to carousing with Martha. On such a long road, a few questionable turns may be expected.

Me

I'm sitting here typing at a wobbly, homemade table; a hard, stale tortilla functions as a shade on the lightbulb dangling above the typewriter; I'm barefoot, my last chili pepper still stings my lips, and my shirt stinks of stale sweat. Banana leaves hang right outside my window, with blue-green mountain slopes rising beyond them.

This *me* harbors clear memories of awakening on a fresh, wet morning several weeks ago, here on Alejandro's porch, thrilling to the sound of roosters crowing. The next day, this *me* was touched completely by witnessing some kids playing inside the cocuite tree's shadows. Moreover, I'm the one who for weeks has been the gringo carrying water from the arroyo across Tepetlayo Ridge, and who for nearly a month simply wandered blindly in the mountains, even to the pines of Querétaro. I'm even the one who not so long ago sat here typing that now I wished to find this slope's "deeper stream" and that henceforward I should "transmit significant messages, like a plump, Agua Zarcan spider thumping its golden web."

Neither for you nor for myself have I defined any particular deeper stream; I'm not sure what this says about me; it frightens me a little.

The Jazz of Going Home

Cold rain. In 8:30 P.M. darkness I'm hanging out the bus window, leaving town on the Fronteras bus line. It's the night of the big local election, the night when Tavo wins. Alejandro says the vote went his way, but he speaks to me while staring at the ground. Three hours earlier this Nahuatl man with origins in corn and beans talked with me while cold rain fell hard on my rented tin roof; his Martha had picked today to jilt him; he sat in the tiny handmade chair held together with rusty wire, crying, recalling old words and wounds, especially the betrayal of his wife, and he talked about how old he's getting.

So, here I am, all this going on, and Alejandro comes down to see me off, and I'm hanging out this window looking at Tamazunchale for the last time while firecrackers explode for winner Tavo and orange light reflects on the street's black water.

Past Avocado Alley, past Hotel Tamazunchale, across the one-lane bridge, then north through winding darkness for the last time.

Mariachi trumpets, the driver's sound system's not bad,

traveling through the night, oncoming-headlight-glare, ab-
stract silhouettes, a large crucifix at the windshield's center,
a sticker beneath—of course—the Virgin of Guadalupe, and
those speakers hung in the windshield's upper corners,
there're little lights inside them flashing in time with the
music, brighter when the trumpets soar or the singer holds
forth on the word *amooooooooor.*

Sitting in the darkness I doze on and off thinking about
Alejandro and the rest. Suddenly it's 5:00 A.M., and I have a
crick in my neck; another doze, and at 7:30 A.M. we're cruis-
ing into Monterrey; northern industrial city, rumble-of-street-
traffic, metallic early-morning glint, new construction, odor
of wet concrete and diesel fumes.

Stiff-legged and a little dazed, walking south from Monterrey's bus station on Avenida Pino Suarez, I find a nice park to
sit in. A random bench sets me facing a colonial-style house
across the street with dozens of glossy young women passing
through a door beneath a sign UNIVERSIDAD REGIOMONTANA
DIVISION CIENCIAS DE LA COMUNICATION (HOTELERIA Y TURISMO):
Future ticket agents, these, and hotel desk clerks, each with
Glamour magazine hair-dos; flashy-white smiles beneath nar-
cissist, wet, obsidian eyes; smiles gamely coordinated with
turning-the-head-real-fast-so-the-hair-swings-out-to-fall-just-
right-onto-the-shoulders; bottle-originated raspberry cheeks;
and I know of what perfumes they smell; and now I am on
the outside sour, but inside needing mightily at least one of
them to chastely walk away with a bucket of water on her
head or turn around so that on her back I can see a mecapál
loaded with firewood. Nahuatl—this plastic! Odors of hot
beans and kerosene, mud and chicken shit!

Walking Nuevo Laredo; ninety degrees at 2:00 P.M. Odors
of dust and from somewhere the smell of a man's blue-green
aftershave. My last 300-peso orange soda and some animal

crackers, then the walk across the bridge to Laredo, Texas, U.S.A.

At 5:05 P.M., I call my mother in Kentucky. It frosted up there last night, but she'd covered the tomatoes with plastic. Lots of pears and apples. My Uncle Mike's dying of kidney failure. Since July I have not spoken to a single native English speaker other than twice on the phone, calling Kentucky. Standing here, speaking my native tongue, it's as if I am some kind of traitor. These English words are hard, full of unnecessary fricatives and stops, somehow arrogant, and it just keeps gushing from me in glittering curls like colored aluminum tinsel no-rhythm-of-tortillas-and-beans-lazy-afternoons-then-at-10:00-P.M.-*paseando*-in-the-park-those-warm-wet-night-shadows-beneath-royal-poincianas.

Standing talking with my mother in front of the Iglesia de San Augustin on Zaragoza Street, I see a local forty-year-old Texas chicano pass humbly, bending his head before the church's door, in profound secrecy making the sign of the cross and right here, with my tongue and lips diesel-ricocheting-off-limestone-road-cuts, for a second I choke up, not knowing why.

Index